A CITIZEN'S GUIDE TO
THE CONSTITUTION AND
THE SUPREME COURT

The U.S. Constitution is a blueprint for a free society as well as a source of enduring conflict over how that society must be governed. The competing ways of reading our founding document shape the decisions of the Supreme Court, which acts as the final voice on constitutional questions. This citizen's guide explains the central conflicts that frame our constitutional controversies, written in clear non-academic language to serve as a resource for engaged citizens, both inside and outside of an academic setting.

After covering the main points of conflict in constitutional law, Marietta gives readers an overview of the perspectives from the leading schools of constititional interpretation—Textualism, Common Law Constitutionalism, Originalism, and Living Constitutionalism. He then walks through the points of conflict and competing schools of thought in the context of several landmark cases and ends with advice to readers on how to interpret constitutional issues ourselves.

Morgan Marietta is Assistant Professor in the Department of Political Science at the University of Massachusetts Lowell. He is the author of *A Citizen's Guide to American Ideology* and *The Politics of Sacred Rhetoric*.

CITIZEN GUIDES TO POLITICS AND PUBLIC AFFAIRS
Morgan Marietta and Bert Rockman, Series Editors

Each book in this series is framed around a significant but not well-understood subject that is integral to citizens'—both students and the general public—full understanding of politics and participation in public affairs. In accessible language, these titles provide readers with the tools for understanding the root issues in political life. Individual volumes are brief and engaging, written in short, readable chapters without extensive citations or footnoting. Together they are part of an essential library to equip us all for fuller engagement with the issues of our times.

TITLES IN THE SERIES

**A Citizen's Guide to American Ideology:
Conservatism and Liberalism in Contemporary Politics**
Morgan Marietta

**A Citizen's Guide to the Constitution and the Supreme Court:
Constitutional Conflict in American Politics**
Morgan Marietta

A CITIZEN'S GUIDE TO THE CONSTITUTION AND THE SUPREME COURT

Constitutional Conflict in American Politics

Morgan Marietta

Routledge
Taylor & Francis Group

NEW YORK AND LONDON

First published 2014
by Routledge
711 Third Avenue, New York, NY 10017

Simultaneously published in the UK
by Routledge
2 Park Square, Milton Park, Abingdon, Oxon OX14 4RN

Routledge is an imprint of the Taylor & Francis Group, an informa business

Library of Congress Cataloging in Publication Data
Marietta, Morgan.
    A citizen's guide to the Constitution and the Supreme Court : constitutional
conflict in American politics / Morgan Marietta.
    pages cm. — (Citizen guides to politics and public affairs)
    Includes bibliographical references.
    1. Constitutional law—United States. 2. Judicial review—United States.
    3. United States. Supreme Court. I. Title.
    KF4550.Z9M275 2013
    342.73—dc23
    2013002946

ISBN: 978-0-415-84379-9 (hbk)
ISBN: 978-0-415-84381-2 (pbk)
ISBN: 978-0-203-75577-8 (ebk)

Typeset in Garamond
by EvS Communication Networx, Inc.

Printed and bound in the United States of America by Publishers Graphics,
LLC on sustainably sourced paper.

FOR JORDAN

CONTENTS

TABLES AND FIGURES

A Note on Capitalization and Italics

The capitalization of terms related to the Supreme Court is not uniform in American publications. The rule I have followed is *foremost show respect*. Terms such as the Supreme Court, the Court, and Justices are capitalized, as are the schools of constitutional interpretation such as Living Constitutionalism and Originalism. Italics are employed to emphasize some of the major points and concepts, making the text easier to read. They are also employed to delineate questions (for example, the constitutional question is *Does the document include a right to privacy?*).

ACKNOWLEDGMENTS

This book originated in a class at the University of Georgia in the spring of 2011. The discussions and debates in those sessions shaped this volume into its current form. A group of outstanding students read chapters of the manuscript and met to discuss its progress. Without their many excellent suggestions this would be a much poorer volume. Special thanks go to the sharp minds of

Will Burgess,
Robert Daniel,
Wells Ellenberg,
Stephen Flowers,
Mark Neufeld,
Jett Puckett,
John Shapiro, and
Jordan Stevens.

I am also indebted to Nathaniel Ament-Stone for his valuable commentary; Andrea Briscoe for editing the manuscript; Karli Hedstrom for several invaluable conversations about the Constitution; Heather Hensley for her contributions to my thinking on the common law; Robert Holzbach for cutting the manuscript down to size; Glenn Kent for his comments on each of the chapters; and Kate Tummarello for her insights into the role of premises in constitutional interpretation.

I would also like to thank David Barker, Jeff Condran, Sam DeCanio, and Robert Peluso, as well as Abby Williams and the rest of the clan, including Alix, Dan, Justin, David, and Ken.

My teachers in constitutional law and legal history contributed a great deal to the development of this volume, including Larry Baum, Les Benedict, Bert Carroll, Peter Karsten, and Shannon Smithey.

Many thanks are due to Michael Kerns at Routledge Press, who supported this series and its goal of speaking to a broad audience about essential political questions. My friend and colleague Bert Rockman was also instrumental in making the series possible.

As always, I am indebted to Mark Perlman, who began my journey toward asking the right questions. He is missed as much as he was admired.

The final acknowledgement is the one I most want to make, to the one who made everything different. Because of you this life is more than I had ever dreamed possible. For making this a better book, making mine a better life, and making me a better man, I will be forever thankful. This book, and everything else, is for Jordan.

INTRODUCTION

The Constitution and Bong Hits for Jesus

In American politics everything comes down to the Constitution. No one disputes its status as the basic document that describes our system of government, yet we disagree about what it means. And the Supreme Court is the final voice on its meaning.

This brief volume is about our competing interpretations of the Constitution, focusing on why reasonable people disagree and what is at stake in the Supreme Court's decisions. The book begins by identifying the points of conflict that are at the heart of our divisions over the meaning of the Constitution and ends with some of the most important decisions the Court has made in recent years. The disagreements over the meaning of the Constitution are easier to understand through these real-world controversies. The first case we will discuss—one that illustrates some of the most important aspects of how the Court analyzes constitutional questions—is known as the Bong Hits for Jesus Case.

One of the core skills in describing a constitutional conflict is rendering the *facts of the case.* This is a clear summary that answers the question *Who is suing whom over what?* The perfect rendition is the shortest possible statement that contains *all* the necessary facts, and *no* unnecessary details. It is brief and complete, leading to the constitutional question at hand. The facts of the Bong Hits case begin with the approach of the Winter Olympics in 2002. Runners carried the Olympic Torch across Alaska in its slow progress toward the site of the games at Salt Lake City, Utah. On the day it was scheduled to pass by Juneau-Douglas High School, the principal allowed students out of classes early so they could witness the event. As the torch went by and the news cameras started to roll, an eighteen-year-old student named Joseph Frederick unfurled a fourteen-foot banner across the street from the school, emblazoned with the phrase "Bong Hits 4 Jesus." Deborah Morse, the principal of the high school, tore down the sign and later suspended Frederick from school for five days. He argued that this was illegitimate because it violated his right to free speech. Morse increased the punishment, as high school principals tend to do if you argue with them. Frederick brought suit alleging a violation of the First Amendment of the U.S. Constitution. The constitutional question was *Can a public school limit a student's free speech rights in the context of the Bong Hits banner?* This is a rather specific question, but it is connected to a long line of free speech controversies that are at the heart of our disagreements about the meaning of the Constitution.

Joseph Frederick's story illustrates that any personal or political event in America could become the foundation of a constitutional controversy. When Frederick brought his case to the federal district court in Alaska, the judge upheld the school's actions. In the court's view, his rights had not been violated. But the Circuit Court, or the court of appeal right below the Supreme Court, reversed this decision and sided with Frederick. With rulings supporting both sides of the dispute, this was not an easy case to sort out. The school administrators decided to press on with their position, the Supreme Court agreed to hear the arguments, and the Bong Hits case would have its final resolution. Deborah Morse was now the person bringing the action on behalf of the school, so the case would be known officially as *Morse v. Frederick.*[1]

The nine Justices of the Supreme Court weighed three considerations: the *principles*, the *premises*, and the *precedents*. These are the three aspects of any constitutional case, but how they are understood is a matter of great disagreement. We will look at each of these in detail in the coming chapters as we address the reasons for the strenuous disagreements they inspire. The constitutional *principles* that are in play are sometimes agreed upon among the Justices, but often not. Sometimes the disagreement is over what a certain principle means. Other times it is whether a principle even exists. Some principles, like privacy or federalism, are believed to be in the Constitution by one group of thinkers, but not by another. The *premises* are social facts, not merely the specific facts of the case at hand but the broader perceived realities of our society. Prevailing circumstances that might influence a case, like the prevalence of racism in our society or the degree of threat to our security posed by foreign nations, are understood very differently by different people. And when the Justices of the Court attempt to answer questions of this nature about our social premises they employ very different approaches. The third consideration is *precedent*, or the role of the previous decisions of the Court. The obvious question is whether the Court has ruled on a similar case that can provide guidance on the current problem. The more difficult question is whether we should follow precedents at all. The proper role for the Court's previous decisions—*when they should be followed and when they should not*—is highly disputed. When we apply each of these considerations to the Bong Hits case, its real meaning begins to emerge.

The Principles

In one sense the principle at issue in *Morse* is clear: free speech, as protected by the First Amendment. Frederick was denied the ability to express himself. On the other hand, there are several recognized exceptions to the principle. The First Amendment guarantees that we shall have no law "abridging the freedom of speech, or of the press," but this has never meant that citizens could say anything they wished whenever they liked. Even the purpose of the principle is debated. Many believe that its role is to allow vigorous political debate. We could not have a system of elections that truly represent the views of the public if we cannot discuss things openly without interference. Others believe that free speech applies well beyond politics, or even literal speech, because without it we cannot have progress in science, literature, or art. The most expansive argument is that freedom of expression is a much broader right that has nothing to do with these consequences, but is instead a pure aspect of individual liberty. In this view, the freedom is not dependent on its consequences—either for effective democracy or for social progress—but is an inherent quality of all free-standing humans. Regardless of the position one takes, the principle of free speech is at the heart of how we define our liberties and therefore at the heart of the work of the Court.

Free speech is perhaps the most absolute principle in the entire document. The First Amendment begins, "Congress shall pass no law. ..." This seems to imply that Congress can take *no* action of any kind that limits speech. None of the other amendments is written in so absolutist a fashion. For example, the Fourth Amendment disallows "unreasonable" searches and seizures. What is unreasonable is a matter of judgment, but surely some searches are reasonable and therefore do not violate the Constitution. Even with the clear language of the First Amendment there are still disputes, and the Supreme Court has allowed many exceptions. This seems to illustrate that the Constitution may not be a document of absolutes as much as general principles.

When understanding a constitutional principle, where do we begin? Do we start with the purpose of the principle, determining why it was established and what good it serves? Alternatively, we could examine the exact language of the text, relying on its specific wording regardless of the intent of the writers. Perhaps we should look at what the Supreme Court has said it means in previous rulings. Or do we consider what it has come to mean to our citizens? These are very different approaches, each of which reflects a major school of thought. How the Justices see these questions illustrates their way of reading the Constitution.

The Premises

Many controversial cases turn on a factual dispute that the Court must resolve. However, the critical question is not always apparent at first blush. In the Bong Hits case, one of the first things that many observers wonder is whether the event took place in school. While a student is under the control of public officials—when they are *at school*—the administrators have clear authority. This is *not* the case if those same administrators were to see a student doing something wrong at the mall over the weekend. So, was the banner displayed at school or not? Several questions might frame the answer. Was it during school time? Yes, it was the final period of the school day, so maybe it *was* school. Was it on school property? No, the banner was across the street, so perhaps it was *not* school. But the students had been released only so they could stay nearby to watch the running of the torch, not to go wherever they wanted. So, maybe it is the equivalent of a field trip and therefore still school. The Court did not spend much energy in coming to the conclusion that this final version was the most accurate description of the situation; the school still had jurisdiction over the students and this was not the pivotal fact of the case.

A second factual dispute was the meaning of the banner. What exactly does "Bong Hits 4 Jesus" mean? Is it an argument in favor of the legalization of marijuana? If it is, then it may be a political statement protected under the intent of the First Amendment. Is it a religious statement? If it is an expression of faith (it does mention Jesus), it may be protected under the First Amendment's guarantee that we shall have no law "prohibiting the free exercise" of religion. Both of these arguments faced an uphill battle because early in the legal proceedings Frederick was asked what the banner meant. He said it was a joke. It was simply a prank with no deeper meaning.

Neither the existence of school time nor the meaning of the banner turned out to be the heart of the case. The key disputed fact was *the nature of students*. Free speech rights, as well as other rights such as voting or serving on juries, clearly apply to full legal persons but maybe not to young people, who possess some rights but not all of them. When it comes to free speech, do students hold the same rights as adults or something less? If a forty-year-old man had taken time out of his day to hold up that banner, this would not be a Supreme Court case. The key question is *Are students the same as adults*?

The issue is the nature of *personhood*: Who is a full person with all of the associated rights and who is not? Merely being a human as opposed to being a full legal person is not at all the same thing. This is a crucial concept in dealing with the Constitution and the nature of rights. An important aspect of our legal tradition is that a person must have the capacity to understand and exercise all of their rights. One example of a human who is not a full legal person is someone of limited mental capacity. They have many rights, but not all of them. Children have certain rights, but not all of those of adults. The transition from childhood to adulthood is the thorny part. At what age or status do all of the rights apply? In recent decades our society has relaxed many of the controls on teenagers, allowing them a range of experience and free choice that far exceeds previous generations. So perhaps they are closer to adults. However, in many ways we believe that minors are different and should have greater legal protections, especially in the realm of criminal prosecutions, where their rights are explicitly stronger than those that apply to adults.[2] In some ways teenagers are more adult than ever while in others they enjoy an extended childhood. The degree to which high school students are akin to adults is unclear.

A question of this nature is no longer about the specific facts of the case itself, such as whether Joseph Frederick was or was not at school, but is instead about the surrounding *social facts*. These are not the individual circumstances of the event, but the broad institutions of our society at large, what could be called constitutional *premises* rather than principles. What makes this kind of question more difficult are the shifts that occur in our society. These facts evolve over time. For example, our understanding of women changed radically since the early days of the nation. At that time, women were much closer to the legal category of children, without recognized rights to vote, hold property, or engage in politics as the equals of men. As social attitudes and realities changed, the Court had to decide several evolving aspects of personhood as they became legal controversies. The full standing of women may seem obvious in our current time, after decades of slow change, but understanding social evolutions as they occur—and judging whether they *have actually occurred*—is no small task. It is the role of the Court to sort out some of our thorniest questions of disputed reality.

How the Court decides questions of evolving premises inspires tremendous disagreement. Are students the same as adults? Are women the same as men? Are all minorities the same as whites? Are gay marriages the same as traditional ones? All of these questions of social facts have come before the Court or will do so in the future. From a seemingly simple question of whether a student can be suspended for making a joke, we have arrived at one of the greatest challenges of constitutional interpretation: determining evolving social facts. This is especially true of the nature of personhood, or who has full rights and who does not, the heart of constitutional controversy for over two hundred years.

The Precedents

The Court does not address questions from a blank slate each time they come into conflict. The Justices have the prior decisions of the Court to guide them. These earlier judgments, called *precedents,* set the stage for current cases. Sometimes the stage is crowded and other times barren. Sometimes it is difficult to tell if a past case applies to the new controversy. In legal circles this is called *reasoning by analogy*: is a previous situation similar, or similar enough, to the current one? The broader controversy is not which precedents apply, but *whether we should be following precedents at all*. Some consider the past decisions of the Court to be our best guide to a clear and predictable system of law. Others believe that following previous errors is a grave injustice merely prolonging confusion about the Constitution and its meaning. So do we rely on precedents or not? The Justices of the Court fall along a continuum from *Yes, almost absolutely*, to *No, they mean little*. There is a middle ground, depending on considerations like how long the rule has been in place or how much agreement among the Justices the previous decision commanded (a unanimous ruling of all nine Justices is more powerful than a 5/4 split). Even the strongest opponent of following precedent believes that some were decided correctly, while even the most devout follower of precedent admits that they must be overturned if they violate basic principles of the Constitution. The Court can be—and has been—simply wrong.

In recent years, several free speech disputes have blossomed, even after well-known rulings that seemed to settle the standard for the First Amendment. One of these decisive cases was *Texas v. Johnson*. In 1984, as Ronald Reagan was receiving the Republican nomination for his second presidential campaign, Gregory Lee "Joey Three Guns" Johnson burned an American flag at a demonstration outside the convention hall in Dallas. Texas law took a dim view of flag desecration, and the police arrested Three Guns during his public protest. In a move that illustrates the complexities of constitutional interpretation, one of the noted Justices on the right of the Court, Antonin Scalia, sided with the liberals to uphold Johnson's right to burn even an American flag. Scalia later said, "it made me furious" to not be able to jail the "bearded, scruffy, sandal-wearing guy burning the American flag," but the Constitution did not allow it because his action was a protected political expression. Given that flag burning is one of the actions the American public disapproves of the most, this decision seemed to close the door on many possible restrictions on free speech.

Perhaps the most controversial free speech case in recent years is *Snyder v. Phelps*, which tested the limits of indecent speech in a free society. The case revolves around the infamous leader of the Westboro Baptist Church, Fred Phelps. From their base in Topeka, Kansas, the Phelps family has conducted a long campaign against the public acceptance of homosexuality. Their central tactic is to attract media attention by coordinating provocative events such as picketing funerals. Signs at these protests often display the group's stock phrase, "God Hates Fags," or alternatively that He hates America, Jews, etc. Other popular signs include "Fags Doom Nations," "America is Doomed," or the straight to the point "You're Going to Hell." Their most controversial claim is that God is punishing the United States for embracing same-sex relationships. The punishments include 9/11 and the Iraq War.

In 2006 the group picketed the funeral of Marine Lance Corporal Matthew Snyder, who had been killed in Iraq. The slogans that day included, "Thank God for Dead Soldiers." This spectacle and the church's statements about the fallen Marine burning in Hell were covered extensively in mainstream media. His father sued Phelps for invasion of privacy and intentional infliction of emotional distress. Albert Snyder argued in court that the Westboro Baptist Church "turned this funeral into a media circus and they wanted to hurt my family. They wanted their message heard and they didn't care who they stepped over. My son should have been buried with dignity." The jury agreed, awarding Snyder substantial monetary damages, roughly half in compensation for his suffering and the other half in what are called punitive damages, designed to punish defendants for their behavior and discourage others. Phelps contested the verdict as a violation of free speech.

The Supreme Court's role was to decide whether Phelps' actions must be allowed under our Constitution regardless of how offensive they are. The Court has recognized several specific exceptions for speech that is not protected by the First Amendment. One is known as the *fighting words doctrine*, first recognized in 1942 in *Chaplinsky v. New Hampshire*. Walter Chaplinsky was arrested for calling a town marshal a "God-damn racketeer" and a "damn fascist." The second insult may not sound so bad, but during a World War against fascism people didn't take kindly to it. Fighting words were defined by the Court as expressions "which by their very utterance inflict injury or tend to incite an immediate breach of the peace." In other words, a reasonable person would likely feel compelled to hit the offender. One question in *Phelps* was whether signs like "Thank God for Dead Soldiers" displayed at the Marine's funeral were fighting words likely to incite reasonable people to violence and therefore are beyond the protections of the First Amendment.

Several other recognized exceptions to free speech are much more common and important. In no particular order they are *obscenity*, *incitement*, *libel*, and *national security*. Obscenity is hard to define, but as one Justice famously said, "I know it when I see it." The Court has agreed throughout our history that obscene or vulgar material is not protected, though what exactly crosses the line is a matter of dispute. Public disruption is also not protected speech. The famous legal example is "shouting *fire* in a crowded theater." This kind of speech creates a danger for others and therefore can be restricted. Language encouraging violence, or in the Court's phrase "inciting or producing imminent lawless action" is outside the bounds of constitutional protection. Lying about someone else in a way calculated to cause harm, what is known as *libel* if in print or *slander* in speech, is also not protected. It may be speech, but it isn't free, given that juries can award sizeable damages for intentionally hurtful lies. Another major exception is the revelation of information harmful to national security. But even this is a limited avenue for government action, as the current rulings limit this to speech that causes foreseeable direct harm before the government can intervene.

These standards apply to adults with all of the legal rights of full citizens. However, the Bong Hits case raises the question of whether free speech rights apply equally to students. Do they have lesser rights to free speech or rights comparable to those of adults? The Supreme Court has addressed the speech rights of students before, including the *Tinker* case in 1969, the most influential of the school speech rulings. A small group of students in Des Moines, Iowa, wore black armbands to protest the Vietnam War. The administrators attempted to stop them and the controversy wound up at the Supreme Court. The Court ruled that if political speech disrupts the teaching mission of the school it can be restricted. Because the Justices saw the armbands as *not* essentially disruptive, they had to be allowed.

The second major school speech case did not go to the students. In the *Bethel School District* case in 1986, a student diverged from the approved script while giving a nominating speech for the vice presidency of the student body. He was later suspended from school. The speech in favor of his friend Jeff Kuhlman stated:

> I know a man who is firm. He's firm in his pants, he's firm in his shirt, his character is firm, but most [of] all, his belief in you the students of Bethel, is firm. Jeff Kuhlman is a man who takes his point and pounds it in. If necessary, he'll take an issue and nail it to the wall. He doesn't attack things in spurts. He drives hard, pushing and pushing until finally, he succeeds. Jeff is a man who will go to the very end, even the climax, for each and every one of you. So please vote for Jeff Kuhlman, as he'll never come between us and the best our school can be.

A long pause in the delivery of the final sentence gave it a distinctly sexual connotation. The Supreme Court decided that vulgarity was another standard for restricting student speech, and the suspension stood.

When these two standards are applied to the Bong Hits case, the banner seems unlikely to be considered vulgar but is possibly disruptive. Was the banner a drug reference that administrators could legitimately consider to be disruptive of the school's mission to exclude illegal substances? This might be an obvious question to ask if we accept the *Tinker* precedent. But what if we believe *Tinker* was decided wrongly? Is a precedent we think wrong nonetheless binding? Another way of phrasing this question is *What do you call a mistake made fifty years ago?* One answer is a precedent. If that is the answer, then even a wrongly decided case has weight that we must respect if the system is to have long-term validity. Another possible answer is that a mistake made fifty years ago is a mistake. Wrongly decided cases don't become more right over time. These two views lead in very different directions, creating one of the serious disagreements among the Justices.

The Bong Hits Decision

Does the Constitution protect a questionable banner raised by a high school student, or are public school officials able to restrict those kinds of expressions? Given the disputes over the principles, the premises, and the precedents, it may not be surprising that this was a close decision, with the nine Justices splitting five to four. So who won? This, of course, is not the point. What the Supreme Court decided in 2007 is not necessarily correct, nor does it surely reflect the meaning of the Constitution. It does, however, illustrate the conflicts in interpretation that divide the Court grounded in different readings of the document. Having put it off long enough to make that point, the Court ruled in favor of the school. Students are not recognized as full persons with full speech rights; they have some rights, but fewer than those of adults. Given this ruling about social facts and the school's interest in maintaining a zero-tolerance policy toward drug use, the school was justified in restricting Frederick's speech. The *Tinker* case—which established the disruption standard for allowing school speech restrictions—does not hold in regard to drug references, broadening the scope of public schools to control student expression.

More important than who won is why the Justices disagreed about what the Constitution means. Why did four Justices disagree with the other five? In one sense the dispute was about constitutional principle. Some Justices believed the free speech principle was stronger and less open to exceptions. In another sense the disagreement was about constitutional premise, or whether students are meaningfully different from adults. But how do we know if the Court upheld the correct understanding of the principles and the accurate interpretation of the premises? It is a common mistake to treat the decisions of the Court as synonymous with the meaning of the Constitution. While it is appropriate to grant the Court its due respect, it is not the current view of the Court but the binding meaning of the Constitution that we are after.

The Bong Hits case focused on the social facts of the personhood of students compared to full adults. But it was not about the specific facts. The Court doesn't care about Joseph Frederick or Deborah Morse. It is the meaning of the Constitution that the Justices care about, which will affect countless future cases. One of the phrases found in many decisions of the Court is "the instant case." It means the case under consideration, but in a sense the phrase is a term of denigration. It implies that the case at hand is *merely* the instant case, the case of the moment, which will fade and be irrelevant while the interpretation of the Constitution will remain.

1

THE CORE DISAGREEMENT

How Should We Read the Constitution?

When many people hear of a constitutional question being decided by the Supreme Court, they employ what I call the *New York Times* syllogism. Most media commentators seem to follow this simple view of constitutional interpretation. Like any syllogism it has three parts in the form of two premises and a logical conclusion. The classic example of a syllogism is: (a) all trout are fish; (b) all fish swim; therefore, (c) all trout swim. The *NYTimes* syllogism begins with the premise (a) *my political views are correct.* Most politically motivated citizens have a clear confidence that their ideals are the right ones. The second premise is (b) the Constitution is correct. In our society this is a mainstream and almost unchallenged view. By now you see where this is going: if my political views are correct, and the Constitution is correct, then clearly (c) *the Constitution must agree with my political views*. It is not necessary to delve into it more deeply or consider the text of the document itself given this clear path to its meaning. If you are sure that the Constitution is correct, it must say what you also know is correct, even if it seems not to. This political shortcut is simple and logically complete, but perhaps fatally flawed. It is quite possible that the Constitution does *not* agree with some of your political preferences. This observation is not an insult. The Constitution is meant to set limits, and it may be the case that some of your personal preferences are outside of its bounds. Nor is it an insult that many people with political ideologies on the Left or Right are convinced that their views are surely reflected in the Constitution. Constitutional interpretation is a complex topic that does not receive its due share of public discussion. A brief explanation of the nuances of the Constitution and the Court is a rare thing, which is what this book attempts to provide.

The *NYTimes* syllogism is related to another problematic observation about reading the Constitution. It isn't that the document is complex, which it is. It isn't that it has several parts and can seem contradictory, which it does. The problem is that many people think they know what it says before they read it. American culture includes frequent references to free speech, freedom of religion, and other constitutional ideas. Almost no adult reader approaches the document without preconceived ideas of its content. Many people expect phrases like "the separation of church and state," or "all men are created equal," even though they are not there to be found. It is likely that we heard about the Supreme Court's decisions on our rights and liberties before we read the relevant passages in the Constitution itself. It is unfortunate that we think we know what it says before we start to read it.[3]

The core question that divides Americans over the meaning of our basic document is *How should we read the Constitution?* The question is rarely addressed head on, because it is grounded in competing assumptions that usually remain hidden. All forms of writing, from newspaper articles to novels or poems, have a set of conventions for how they are read or heard. When we see a dateline on a newspaper article (for example: "Washington (AP)—Members of Congress today began ..."), we know what to expect. When we hear "Once upon a time ...," we have a completely different understanding of what we are about to hear. There may be goblins, fairies, quite possibly a princess in danger. But we know that when we hear about the princess being imprisoned in the tower there is no need to call the police because unlike the news story, it isn't real. However, if we did not know the conventions of a bedtime story it would be different. It only makes sense because we know the expected conventions of either story. But imagine if we didn't know them, or worse yet, reversed them.

Reading a novel is much the same in the sense that it relies on knowing the conventions. When the narrator says, "Jones walked down the street, thinking about why his wife just left him," we don't bother to wonder how anyone could possibly know what Jones was thinking, which is clearly impossible. We are accustomed to an omniscient narrator, so we suspend our disbelief. This was not true before the invention of novels. When *Robinson Crusoe* was first published in 1719, written in the form of his diaries on the island, many readers were upset when they learned it was a made up story.[4] News reports, bedtime stories and novels all make sense to us only because we know the conventions, but the Constitution is a unique document that we are not accustomed to reading, so its conventions are unknown to most citizens.

Four Conventions of the Constitution

The conventions of reading the Constitution can be reduced to four simple things that create far-reaching consequences. Some of the conventions are accepted by almost everyone, while others lead to profound disagreements. The first, and least controversial, is that *every word has a specific meaning*. I call this *differentiation*. If the Constitution employs a word in one place, this word means the same thing when used in a different place. If a different word was chosen, it must mean something different. It would be illegitimate to argue that this new word really means the same thing as the first one, because if that were meant to be the case the Founders would have used the first word. In the same vein, the Constitution does not repeat itself. Therefore it would be illegitimate to argue that a given section simply means the same thing as another section. This convention mandates that the Constitution be read as if it were written carefully. The document does not repeat itself any more than it uses words sloppily. Every part, and every word, is differentiated.

In many instances this may seem obvious or unimportant, but occasionally it matters a great deal. The Fourteenth Amendment speaks of due process and equal protection of the laws. But who has these protections? If an illegal immigrant is picked up on U.S. soil, are they guaranteed the equal protection of the laws under the Fourteenth Amendment? Unlike the first part of the Amendment, which speaks of citizens, these clauses speak of *persons*. This suggests that the answer is *Yes*. If the clause had spoken of *citizens*, it may well be *No*, but the word is *persons*. If the Constitution had meant only citizens, it would have said so. Could the Amendment merely reiterate or reinforce previous protections found earlier in the Constitution? No, because the document does not repeat itself. For the same reason, the Ninth Amendment must have a specific meaning, as must the Tenth, which does not merely repeat the Ninth, or any other part of the document. The meaning of these two amendments is a matter of great controversy, as we will discuss later. While it is tempting for many readers to construe certain passages as if they really implied other words, or as if they merely repeated other passages, the convention of differentiation tells us that this would be wrong.

The second convention is that the Constitution must be read *chronologically.* Our Constitution is designed to be an alterable document. It contains provisions for new amendments and has been altered significantly at different points in our history. Later parts sometimes eradicate or change the meaning of earlier parts. These changes can have clear ramifications, but at other times the new meaning of the older text is not obvious. Some of the uncontroversial changes include alcohol, taxes, and election laws. If we stopped reading after the Eighteenth Amendment, we would be surprised by the amount of alcohol flowing through our cities and college campuses. But the legal alcohol trade was restored by the Twenty First Amendment fourteen years later. Likewise, the powers denied to Congress in Article I seem to clearly include levying an income tax, which would make our whole system of federal taxation impossible were it not for the Sixteenth Amendment, which allowed for income taxes after 1913. When Article I speaks of the Senate, it clearly says that senators will be chosen by state legislators, placing a buffer between the people and the selection of the upper house of Congress. Our current system of elections would make no sense without knowing that the Seventeenth Amendment changed the Senate into a popularly elected body like the House of Representatives in order to increase the influence of ordinary voters.

These changes are important, but it is really the Fourteenth Amendment that is the prime example of how reading chronologically leads to controversial conclusions. Most Americans believe that the First Amendment means that their local or state governments cannot restrict citizens' rights to free speech. They are not wrong, but that is not what the First Amendment says. It says that the *Congress* cannot restrict free speech rights, but says nothing about the local authorities who are more likely to do so. The Fourteenth Amendment changed the meaning of the earlier amendments to include all forms of government, but this is impossible to know just reading the First Amendment alone. The changes that the Fourteenth Amendment brought about are controversial even today, with different Justices of the Court taking very different positions about exactly how the later amendment changed how we should read the earlier ones. This is one of the great points of conflict in constitutional interpretation—exactly how the nature of rights under the Constitution changed with the Fourteenth Amendment—which we will discuss in Chapter 3.

The third convention could be described as *balancing*. Easy cases do not get to the Supreme Court. And the hard cases usually have strong arguments on either side. Often they each have support from different aspects of the Constitution. This is possible because the document is contradictory in important ways. Our form of democracy can be understood as a fundamental contradiction between majority rule— the basic definition of democracy—and individual rights that the majority cannot violate. The majority rules, except when it can't. This, of course, makes no sense. Much of the Constitution establishes the process by which the public can achieve its will, but other parts limit that capacity. This may create a principled system with positive long-term outcomes for citizens, but that doesn't help us resolve any specific contradiction. For example, Article II of the Constitution gives the president control of the armed forces and the power to direct them during times of public danger. The Fourth Amendment says that the executive power to seize or detain citizens in an attempt to protect the public is limited. So, if the president claims that Article II empowers him to act against a citizen, but that person claims the Fourth Amendment prohibits it, which part of the document trumps the other part? No doubt some sort of balancing is in order, but how that balancing is to be achieved leads to great disputes.

The *differentiation* of each word or phrase in the Constitution is agreed upon by almost all readers; and a *chronological* reading is widely accepted; and *balancing* is understood in principle even if causing conflict in practice. The fourth convention—reading the document *comprehensively*—creates the greatest controversy. In his influential book *The Bill of Rights* (published in 1998), Yale Law School Professor Akhil Amar argues that the way law schools teach the Constitution has stripped it of its real meaning: "Instead of being studied holistically, the Bill [of Rights] has been broken up into discrete blocks of text, with each segment examined in isolation ... When we move beyond law school classrooms to legal scholarship, a similar pattern emerges. Each clause is typically considered separately." But "how could we forget that our Constitution is a single document, and not a jumble of disconnected clauses?"[5] Another famous book in legal circles is *The Least Dangerous Branch*, written by Alexander Bickel in 1962. He also argues that "of course, the document must be read as a whole, and any particular phraseology is informed by the purpose of the whole."[6] Nonetheless, the convention of reading the Constitution comprehensively is highly disputed, not merely because most readers are accustomed to only looking for specific passages, but because a comprehensive approach can lead to more problematic conclusions.

If we read the Constitution comprehensively, then we can understand it comprehensively as well. The whole can mean more than the sum of its parts. This approach is known as *transcendence*, reading the Constitution for its overarching meaning. If we read the document like a novel, then perhaps we can discern broad themes. For almost any novel, a reader can offer a summary of its meaning: *Pride & Prejudice* (or almost any Jane Austen novel) argues that social convention and personal happiness are at odds; *Romeo & Juliet* means that love is eternal (or perhaps that it will get you killed). If we read the Constitution in a similar fashion, does it contain transcendent principles? Transcendence is embraced by some commentators, but rejected strenuously by others. If we can identify specific principles that define the document and rise above any specific clause or phrase, this creates a very different perspective than one that limits us to the literal meaning of the words. The dispute over this possible convention is one of the points of conflict to be discussed below.

Four Schools of Interpretation
(or Ways of Reading the Constitution)

The conventions of reading the Constitution moved quickly from consensus to conflict. This is only a starting point for the broader disagreements over alternative ways of reading the document. Competing approaches to the act of reading are discussed in college English departments throughout America. Without going too deeply into the vitriolic debates of literature scholars, there are at least four clearly identifiable approaches to reading a text:

1. We seek the meaning or purpose of the author.

2. We examine the exact language of the text, which has a precise and distinguishable meaning independent from the author's intent or a reader's biases.

3. We look at what previous readers and interpreters have believed it means, which suggests that what has been said about a text may be more important than the text itself.

4. We consider what it has come to mean to contemporary readers.[7]

These ways of reading apply to the Constitution as much as to any other document. One of these four approaches is at the heart of each of the four major schools of constitutional interpretation, except we call them *Originalism, Textualism, Common Law Constitutionalism,* and *Living Constitutionalism.* Each of these schools of thought will receive a great deal of attention in later chapters, but they reduce to simple ways of reading the Constitution which mirror the approaches found in studies of literature:

1. For any given constitutional principle, we start with the purpose of that principle, determining why it was established and what good it serves. From an *Originalist* perspective, the author is the authority on the meaning of a text, in this case the Founders themselves.

2. We examine the exact language of the text and argue that it means what the specific wording states regardless of the intent of the writers. *Textualists* concentrate on the words themselves, not the authors or readers.

3. We look at what the Supreme Court has said it means in the past. *Common Law Constitutionalists* take the history of the Court's decisions to be the most important guide to the meaning of the document.

4. We consider what it has come to mean to contemporary citizens. *Living Constitutionalists* emphasize the ambiguous and shifting nature of language as well as the need to adapt interpretations to the values and perceptions of current readers.

Constitutional disputes are grounded in these ways of reading. Whether a given reader—a Supreme Court Justice, lawyer, or citizen—accepts one view or another depends on the answers to a series of smaller questions that add up to an allegiance to one approach. When the arguments are broken down into their most clear divisions, I count *nine distinct points of conflict* over how to interpret the Constitution. With these points of conflict in mind, the schools of thought become easily understandable. More importantly, once we take a position on each of these divisions, the matching school of thought becomes clear. These nine concepts—coincidentally the same number as there are Justices of the Supreme Court—form the building blocks necessary to understand and interpret the Constitution. The following chapters address each of these divisions. One does not need to be a lawyer or a specialist in constitutional law to understand them. But assuming that the Justices of the Supreme Court think just like politicians or other ideologically motivated people will not do. The important question is what beliefs are at play in their minds rather than just ours. This takes us into a new and fascinating terrain regarding how to read the Constitution. In order to simplify it, we will concentrate on the nine central points of conflict in turn, leading up to the major schools of interpretation, or the disputed ways of reading our basic text.

Part I

POINTS OF CONFLICT

2

JUDICIAL REVIEW

Is It Legitimate and Expansive, or Questionable and Limited?

The nine Justices of the Supreme Court are divided by an equal number of major disputes over how they read the Constitution. These points of conflict are listed in Table 2.1 below. Most are related to the facets of any legal case discussed in the introduction: the principles, the premises, and the precedents. Five conflicts are about principles, one is about premises, and one is about precedents. While the larger share deals with principles, the controversies over social facts and historical precedents are also crucial. The two remaining conflicts center on broad questions about the entire enterprise of reading the Constitution: *Who gets to decide what it means?* and *What else (if anything) do we need to read?*

Americans have accepted the Supreme Court's role in determining the meaning of our core document, but the extent of the Court's power is a matter of great controversy. The first point of conflict in understanding the Constitution is the nature of *judicial review*, or the judgment of whether government acts are unconstitutional. Courts around the world often judge whether something is lawful or unlawful, fair or unfair. But whether something is constitutional or unconstitutional—in accord with our basic document or outside of its bounds—is a less-obvious question. We have all heard the mantra that the legislative branch makes the laws, the executive branch enforces the laws, and the Supreme Court determines what is constitutional. This seems obvious to us over two hundred years after the Founding, but it was not clear in the early days of the nation. Instead, the Supreme Court's power grew over time, which may or may not be the ideal arrangement. Whether we needed a single institution to determine constitutionality—or more

Table 2.1 Nine Points of Constitutional Conflict

Overarching Question 1:	*Judicial Review* (who gets to interpret the Constitution?)
Principles:	*Rights, Federalism, Liberty, Religion, Transcendence*
Premises:	*Social Facts*
Precedents:	*Following Precedent*
Overarching Question 2:	*Completeness* (what else do we need to read?)

importantly whether the Supreme Court is the right body to fill that role—is the heart of the dispute. The question may seem to be settled in the affirmative on both counts, but that masks a deep and lingering division over the legitimacy of judicial review. The dispute is not about a principle in the Constitution, but instead about how we decide questions of principle. It is about *who* reads the Constitution as much as it is about *how* to read the Constitution. Who has the power to decide if a government act is out of bounds and therefore void? How broad or narrow should that power be? Should it be used often or rarely, and what justification is required? One camp sees judicial review as an obvious and necessary feature of our politics, deserving a broad role. Another camp grudgingly admits its necessity, but sees it as dangerous and counter to the spirit of democracy, which reserves power primarily to the people and their representatives rather than to unelected judges. Judicial review is either legitimate and expansive, or questionable and limited.

The Institutions of the Court

When historians say that the power of judicial review developed during our history, it often sounds as if this were inevitable. But the establishment of judicial review was the product of calculated acts of specific leaders, without whom it may have evolved differently. The Constitution establishes the judicial branch in Article III, following the discussion of the Congress and the presidency. The legislative branch receives the longest and most detailed attention, while Article III is by far the briefest description allotted to any of the three branches of our government. It merely places "the judicial power" in the hands of the Supreme Court, with little clarification. The Justices of the Supreme

Court are appointed by the president, confirmed by the Senate, and serve until their voluntary retirement. These three aspects of the Court are established by the Constitution, but that is where it falls silent. The contemporary institutions of the Court are supported more by tradition than by constitutional command. We have nine Justices, but that number has varied over time and is not mandated by the Constitution. President Franklin Roosevelt attempted to increase the number in the 1930s, in what is known as the Court Packing incident, but FDR's maneuver to stack the bench with Justices who shared his politics was rejected by an angry public and the number has been settled since then. Judicial review emerged through an act of the Court itself in the early days of the Republic and evolved over the last two hundred years into its current form.

The process of a Supreme Court decision begins when an aggrieved party believes there has been a constitutional error at the lower courts, as Deborah Morse (the principal of Juneau-Douglas High School) did in the Bong Hits case. At this point, the case has already been heard at least twice. The first time was at the original trial court and the second time on appeal to a higher court, such as a federal Circuit Court (if a federal law is at issue) or a State Supreme Court (if it involves a state law).[8] The vast majority of legal cases have no constitutional aspect, but those that do may be considered one final time.

One of the things that surprise many Americans about the Supreme Court is that the Justices control the selection of cases. Accepting a case is called granting *certiorari* (SER-shee-o-RARE-ree), often contracted as simply granting cert (sert). The Justices only take the appeals they choose to and are under little obligation to hear any specific case appealed from a lower court. If they decline to hear a case, then the prior ruling stands. The Court hears about a hundred cases each year (which is roughly 1% of the requests they receive), though this number varies depending on current events and the attitudes of the Justices. They follow what is called the Rule of Four: if four of the nine Justices choose to hear a case it goes on the docket, or the list of upcoming cases. The reasons they choose or decline specific cases are not clear, nor do they have to provide a justification. They are more likely to take a case if it addresses a conflict among the federal circuit courts, for example if a different rule is in place in California (the 9th Circuit) and Georgia (the 11th Circuit).

Once a case is accepted, it is scheduled for oral argument. Each side is given a half hour to argue their case to the bench and individual Justices have the opportunity to interrupt with questions. Some are very active in pressing the lawyers, while others rarely speak (Justice Clarence Thomas has gone for many years without asking a single question). The value of these sessions is sometimes doubted, but it is a tradition of the Court. After oral arguments have been heard, the Justices meet in a private conference to discuss their positions. The initial vote gives the Chief Justice a sense of which side has a majority, but the more important step is the next one of writing the opinion of the Court. The critical issue is not just who wins, but instead the reasoning behind the decision and the legal standard that is established. Placing this in writing for public consumption is a core aspect of the Court's duties. If the Chief Justice is in the majority, he assigns a member of that group (possibly himself) to write the opinion. If the Chief is in the minority, the most senior Justice in the majority group makes that assignment. The writing of the opinion can take weeks or months, as the drafts circulate among the Justices and various members sign on. Often there is a process of negotiation over exactly which standard will be announced or how it will be phrased.

While the majority opinion is being written, the Justices in the minority are also discussing and writing their own reasoning, in what are known as *dissenting opinions* or simply *dissents*. A powerful and well-reasoned dissent can have important long-term influence. Writing a dissent for the purpose of giving future Justices the grounds for overturning a decision—as well as memorable quotes to employ—is referred to as "burying bones." If a Justice agrees with the outcome of who wins the case but disagrees about the reasoning, he can write a *concurrence* or *concurring opinion*, expressing his own reasoning about the proper constitutional rule.

None of these procedures—the Rule of Four, the oral arguments, the assignment of authorship by seniority—are mandated by the Constitution. They are not constitutional commands, but simply conventions that have been developed and agreed upon by the Justices over time. They may or may not be the most optimal or justifiable set of rules. They could be changed at any time, but have the force of tradition behind them. Occasionally a movement arises within the legal community to alter some of these procedures, often to increase or restrict the number of Justices and the number of cases that are heard. These are implicit arguments that judicial review is important and should be expanded or that it is questionable and should be more limited. Which of these views should prevail is controversial, especially given the origins of the practice. Judicial review did not derive from the Constitution nor from an act of Congress, but through a decision of the Supreme Court itself.

Marbury v. Madison

Considered one of the greatest legal minds in American history, Chief Justice John Marshall was a brilliant politician as well as the founder of judicial review. His legacy is intertwined with the story of what is considered the great case in American constitutional history, *Marbury v. Madison*. The facts of the case begin with the election of Thomas Jefferson in the presidential contest of 1800. This was before the establishment of organized political parties, but nonetheless our early leaders had gravitated into two camps: the Federalists, led by Hamilton and Adams, and the Democratic Republicans (not to be confused with either the current Democratic or Republican party), led by Jefferson and Madison. The Federalists had held sway for the first twelve years of the Republic under George Washington and then John Adams. But in 1800 the politics swung toward the Jeffersonians, who favored a weaker national government compared to the aims of the Federalists. As the first unfriendly change of administration in American history, there was no precedent about how the peaceful transfer of power was to take place. In the days before his departure, President Adams made a number of "midnight appointments" of new federal judges and local magistrates. One of these positions was to go to William Marbury as a Justice of the Peace in Washington, D.C. But several of the new appointments, though signed by President Adams, had not been physically delivered to the new judges. They were left on the desk of the incoming Secretary of State, James Madison. After some consideration, Madison simply declined to deliver the new papers, effectively keeping the new judges out of office. Marbury was understandably upset. He sued, claiming that his right to the appointment had been violated. Specifically, he asked the Supreme Court to issue a Writ of Mandamus (man-DAY-muss), an order for a government officer to fulfill a duty, in this case Madison's duty to deliver the appointment.

We now have most of the cast of characters in place. The outgoing President was John Adams. The incoming President was Thomas Jefferson. The incoming Secretary of State was James Madison, who was sued by the newly appointed but unfulfilled Justice of the Peace, William Marbury. But who was the outgoing Secretary of State who had neglected to deliver the new appointments? It was John Marshall. Later, as the Chief Justice of the Supreme Court, he was called upon to rule on his own mistake. Today this would be considered an obvious conflict of interest and the Justice would remove himself from the case, but in the early days of the nation such expectations had not developed. This detail is crucial to understanding the case and its resolution, because everyone expected that Marshall would rule in Marbury's favor: both men were Federalists and granting Marbury the appointment would correct Marshall's own error.

The decision in *Marbury* proceeds in a clear and regimented fashion, which has been emulated by Justices ever since. Marshall poses and answers three questions that he argues settle the case. The first is *Does Marbury have a right to the commission?* Marshall answers *Yes.* Clearly Marbury had been selected, the papers had been signed by the proper authorities, and he had a right to receive them. So far, so good for Marbury. The second question is *Do the laws provide a remedy?* Again, Marshall answers in the affirmative. An old common law action—the Writ of Mandamus requested by Marbury—is appropriate and within the judicial power of the Court. Things are looking very good for the new magistrate. The final question is *Can the Supreme Court issue the Writ?* Marshall's answer is *No.* Regardless of Marbury's legitimate claim and the available remedy, the Court has no power to intervene. Marshall concludes that Marbury relied upon a Congressional Act— the Judiciary Act of 1789—which violated the Constitution and was therefore void. The Judiciary Act had increased the jurisdiction of the Supreme Court beyond the bounds established by Article III of the Constitution. For nearly all matters, the Constitution states that the high court is only for appeals, not for hearing cases as they first come to trial. But Marbury had brought his action immediately to the Supreme Court, as directed by the new rules established by Congress. According to Marshall, this procedure violates the Constitution and must be struck down, so the Court has no power to issue the Writ as Marbury deserves.

In this brilliant stroke, by denying himself the power to do something everyone knew he wanted, Marshall established the broader power of judicial review. This was not the first time the power had been conceptualized or discussed, but it was the first time judicial review was exercised against the Congress, clearly stated by the Supreme Court, and accepted in our politics.[9] In two famous phrases he convinced his contemporaries of these dual propositions: 1) that "a law repugnant to the Constitution is void," and 2) "It is emphatically the province and duty of the judicial department to say what the law is." The first idea is that judicial review must exist under our system. The second is that it must be performed by the Supreme Court. Though both concepts were controversial when they were announced (and are not entirely accepted even now), Marshall won his points by losing. He gave away the Federalist commission for Marbury but established judicial review, a substantial increase in the power of the national government. Imagine for a moment that he had taken the more direct approach, declaring the power of judicial review in a case that would claim a victory for his own party. It would have been seen as fraudulent. But to win by losing was genius. In one of the most brilliant political moves in early American history, Marshall expanded the power of the Supreme Court against the wishes of the sitting president and altered our understanding of the Constitution.

The Continuing Controversy of Judicial Review

To see why Marshall's maneuver was questionable, and why judicial review is still a matter of controversy, we need only ask a few questions. If we emulate Marshall by posing the key questions about his decision in the same fashion that he did about Marbury's lawsuit, perhaps they are:

1. *Did the Judiciary Act of 1789 clearly violate the Constitution?*
2. *Is it clear under the Constitution that we must have judicial review performed by the Supreme Court?*
3. *If judicial review is weaker and employed less frequently, what power is increased instead?*

The answers to these questions explain the continuing controversy. The last one is especially important, because it explains the division between contemporary liberals and conservatives over an expansive judicial review.

Beginning with the first question, *Did the Judiciary Act of 1789 clearly violate the Constitution?* Marshall employs this vehicle to establish judicial review, so it raises serious questions about the origins of the practice. *Marbury* is thought of as the great constitutional decision, but not because of the excellence of its reasoning on this score. Marshall interprets the Constitution's statements on judicial power quite oddly. The relevant passage seems to be Article III, Section 2:

> In all cases affecting ambassadors, other public ministers and consuls, and those in which a state shall be party, **the Supreme Court shall have original jurisdiction.** In all the other cases before mentioned, the Supreme Court shall have appellate jurisdiction, both as to law and fact, **with such exceptions, and under such regulations as the Congress shall make.** (bold added for emphasis)

Isn't the Judiciary Act, which expanded the original jurisdiction of the Court, an example of "such exceptions ... as the Congress shall make"? In this sense, the problem is not obvious. So was the Judiciary Act a clear violation of the Constitution? *No.* Ruling as Marshall did requires an extremely restrictive reading of the final expansive clause. Is there a principled reason to read the document in this fashion? Only if we follow a narrow understanding of the powers inherent in all branches of the federal government even when provisions for their expansion are provided. This was not Marshall's usual perspective, nor is it natural to a neutral reader. While Marshall's reading of the Constitution on the Supreme Court's jurisdiction is remarkably strict, his reading of its implied powers regarding judicial review is remarkably broad, relying on what the document seems to imply or logically require. He allowed a restrictive reading of judicial jurisdiction to facilitate an expansive reading of judicial power. The original case establishing judicial review is a weak foundation for such a great principle.

Moving to the second question, *Is it clear under the Constitution that we must have judicial review performed by the Supreme Court?*

Marshall is adamant on this point, and he is supported by Alexander Hamilton in the *Federalist Papers*, which are taken to be an authoritative commentary on the ratification debates about the meaning of the Constitution. In *Federalist 78*, Hamilton argues that the rights recognized under the Constitution "can be preserved in practice no other way than through the medium of *courts of justice*, whose duty it must be to declare all *acts contrary to the manifest tenor of the Constitution void*. Without this, all the reservations of particular rights or privileges would amount to nothing" (italics added for emphasis).[10] Neither Hamilton nor Marshall rely on the text of the Constitution, but instead on the logic of the system it designs. Protected rights mean little without a means to protect them.

If we agree with Marshall that judicial review is necessary, this still does not tell us who ought to fill that role. While Marshall is persuasive about the question he asks—*do we need judicial review?*—he is much less persuasive about the question he mostly dodges, which is *who should do it?* A part of Hamilton's justification in the *Federalist Papers* is that the Supreme Court, in his famous phrase, is "the least dangerous" branch. It has "no influence over either the sword or the purse" meaning it does not have the military power of the president nor the taxation power of the Congress.[11] The Court cannot enforce its own decisions, which means that it must be persuasive and offer legitimacy. The Justices have no power to compel, but only judgment and intellect to convince. However, the power and profile of the Court have clearly grown over the last two hundred years, especially in the decades following World War II. Hamilton may have become increasingly mistaken about the judiciary being the least powerful branch.

Why should the Supreme Court alone wield this power? Are the Justices the only ones suited to read and understand the Constitution? All senators and members of Congress also swear to support and defend the Constitution, as do the president and all of his deputies, including the attorney general. Are they less capable of understanding and upholding it? Moreover, they are elected (or serve at the discretion of the president) and can be removed if they violate this trust, while Justices cannot be voted out of office, opening up the possibility that they can abuse their authority with little consequence. The most common justification for the Court's power is that Congress cannot be trusted to determine the constitutionality of laws that it has passed—the foxes must not guard the henhouse. We must have checks and balances against national power. But if we must have checks and balances, why does the Supreme Court sit at the top of the hierarchy? Who will check them?

Another common defense of the Supreme Court's position as the final check in the system is the Supremacy Clause. Article VI of the Constitution states:

> This Constitution, and the laws of the United States which shall be made in pursuance thereof; and all treaties made, or which shall be made, under the authority of the United States, **shall be the supreme law of the land**; and **the judges in every state** shall be bound thereby, anything in the Constitution or laws of any State to the contrary notwithstanding.

The problem is that this passage does not mention the Supreme Court as the actor. If we follow the first convention of reading the Constitution—that it was carefully written, with each word having positive meaning—then why does it not mention the Supreme Court? Nor does it mention acts of Congress as objects of judicial review, but instead focuses on state laws, specifically mentioning "the judges in every state" as the entities that are bound by the Constitution. Clearly the parts are subordinate to the whole, or the states to the federal government. Acts of Congress, on the other hand, may be exactly "the laws of the United States" described in the clause as being supreme. The Supremacy Clause says nothing about who should conduct judicial review or what branches of the national government fall under its purview. In the end, Marshall does not provide much of a justification for the Supreme Court's sole possession of constitutional review.

An important argument in favor of the Supreme Court's role comes from Alexander Bickel, an influential legal scholar and noted supporter of a specific form of judicial review. His argument is that the Court is the only agent qualified to conduct this vital function, but only if it wields its unchecked power in a limited way. The Court is the only institution that can uphold the core constitutional values of the nation regardless of current politics. In this sense, judicial review is the "process of enunciating and applying certain enduring values of our society," and the Supreme Court must be "the pronouncer and guardian of such values."[12] Only the Court can do this because only the Justices have the time and temperament to focus on this mission alone. More importantly, they are free to do so because they are unelected. Bickel argues that only an *unelected* group can defend the Constitution, specifically because they are not beholden to current whims of our citizens. But neither are the Justices free agents. The Court's role is to represent our *true selves* rather than our *current selves*. Our true selves believe in the core values of the American endeavor, which are expressed in the Constitution. Our true selves are our constitutional selves. In this sense the document is an organic expression of our values, written by and for us. If our current selves diverge from the values of the Constitution, we must be reminded that *we* are wrong, and *it* is not. It is a reflection of our better selves. The document and its values are ours in a permanent and unchangeable way. Therefore a specific institution, unelected by our current selves but instead with the judgment necessary to understand our true selves, must stand guard.

This perspective presents a core question of our democracy: can the majority of the people override the binding values of our founding document? Or are the values of our origins supreme, more important than the changing values of our people? Is our democracy one of current majorities or enduring values? For some, the idea that our people are restrained against their own wishes is undemocratic, even authoritarian. For others, core values are the essence of who we are, designed as a bulwark against temporary passions or errors. Those who accept Bickel's argument see in judicial review a necessary protection of the Founding values expressed in the Constitution. For those who are uncomfortable with the existence of our true selves and their binding force on our current desires, the justification for judicial review is less clear.

Bickel's position is a defense of judicial review by the Supreme Court, but also an argument for its limits. Judicial review is valid, but only for protecting the clear values of the Founding. The limits of the Court are expressed in the *Rule of Obvious Error*. Under this rule, the Justices should override an act of the people's representatives *only if it clearly violates the Constitution*. Rather than employ their own judgment as if they were legislators, Justices should give the benefit of the doubt to lawmakers. The Court's role is not to replace legislative judgment with judicial judgment. Only when a constitutional principle is manifest and its violation is evident should the Justices overrule the actions of another branch of our government.[13]

We can now see the heart of the disagreement over judicial review: is it an expansive or restricted power? The disagreement is perhaps revealed best by the answer to the last of the three questions posed earlier. *If judicial review is weaker and employed less frequently, what power is increased instead?* When judicial review is more limited, power in our society resides with the majority of the people. Legislative acts passed by the people's representatives receive more deference and are less likely to be overturned. The alternative to a robust judicial review is majoritarian democracy, the focus of most of the Constitution. The balance between majority rule and individual rights is a permanent tension, but the more judicial review expands, the lesser the role of the majority of citizens. A more limited judicial review promotes a greater role for citizen politics.

Once the question is raised, it is not obvious that judicial review is entirely legitimate or more importantly who should perform it. So is judicial review a total fraud, a mad power grab by the Supreme Court? This is no doubt stating the argument too strongly. Few contemporary observers doubt that our constitutional system requires some exercise of judicial review by the Court. The real debate is about self-restraint and the role of representative democracy. Relying on judicial review to solve our problems may infantilize the public and therefore the democratic process. It replaces a robust public discussion and involvement in our political decisions with control by nine Justices who are far removed from normal citizens. If the essence of the Constitution is the empowerment of citizen politics, then the institution of judicial review may be necessary but limited in scope. The opposing view is that only an expansive judicial review can protect individual rights from the power of tyrannical majorities. Without an active judiciary, individual liberties may expand only slowly, if at all.

This division explains the meaning of the term *judicial activism*, which is often employed by more conservative thinkers as a description of many contemporary decisions of the Supreme Court. It refers to the power of courts replacing the judgment of Congress or state governments. Contemporary conservatives tend to trust the people to get it right, acting through their representatives. This suggests that the Supreme Court should disregard the will of the people only if there is a clear and substantial violation of the Constitution (the rule of obvious error). Contemporary liberals, on the other hand, tend to believe that the majority will tend to violate the rights of individuals and minorities, whether through an intent to dominate or a simple lack of awareness of the claims of people different from themselves. In this view, the Constitution intends for the majority to be thwarted in these circumstances by a Supreme Court empowered by an expansive judicial review. Some call a broad role for the Supreme Court judicial activism, while others call the same thing the legitimate and necessary power of the Supreme Court in a functioning democracy. This is no small disagreement at the heart of competing ways of understanding our political system. It is our first point of conflict among readers of the Constitution.

3

RIGHTS

Are They Individual or Collective?

The language of rights is a normal part of our political conversation, yet we disagree in important ways about what they are. We agree that rights are what lawyers call "a recognized privilege or immunity."[14] Unlike most of our political decisions that can be altered as our people and legislatures change their minds, rights are protected and immutable. They either empower us to commit certain actions (a privilege) or protect us from specific government action (an immunity). This sounds well and good until we realize that the power to act and the ability to resist actions can be directly contradictory. If we have political rights to control our environment (privileges) but other people have rights to not be controlled (immunities), who has the upper hand? The heart of the dispute is not whether privileges trump immunities or the reverse, but instead *who holds the right?* If we, the *collective* people of the Constitution, hold the right, then we can act in a democratic fashion based on the will of the majority, but if we, the *individual* people of the Constitution hold the right, then we can resist the decisions of the majority. Different answers to the question of collective versus individual rights have an immediate impact on which actions are constitutional or unconstitutional.

One way to explain the concept of collective rights is to start with the observation that our most central democratic rights empower us as a group rather than as individuals. First and foremost under the Constitution we have the right to elect our representatives. More than an individual right to vote, it is a collective right to control our destiny. The Bill of Rights also deals as much with collective rights as individual ones. The First Amendment protects five rights: speech, press, religion, assembly, and petition. The right to assemble for political purposes (in a party, social movement, or interest group) is a collective right, as is the right to petition for grievances. Both were designed to protect our group right to control the government. Freedom of the press is the right to have access to the free flow of political information; it is a collective right to available knowledge more than an individual right to publish a newspaper. Freedom of religion is the collective right of congregations as well as the individual right of worshippers.

The other amendments of the Bill of Rights also invoke majoritarian rights. The Second Amendment right to bear arms is a collective right to form an armed militia as well as an individual right to protect one's home. The Sixth and Seventh Amendment rights to juries were seen by the Founders as more collective than individual. The jury right in particular is worth discussing because in the early days of the Republic it was seen as a foundational political right. Today we see a jury trial as primarily a bulwark against a mistaken guilty verdict. The Founders saw this right as a protection against political domination by the government. Under the rule of the British monarch, one of the common forms of eliminating opponents of the regime was to charge them with crimes in order to have them removed, temporarily or permanently. The Crown controlled the courts, so a false guilty verdict was easy enough to arrange. This is one of the reasons we have an independent judiciary and is also the origin of the right of trial by jury. Any accusation of a crime must be upheld by a group of local citizens, allowing politically motivated prosecutions to be rejected by a jury. This protection has been so successful in ruling out prosecutions designed to destroy political enemies of the government that we have largely forgotten its purpose, but the jury right is at heart a collective protection of our ability to engage in political opposition. To summarize these observations, several parts of the Bill of Rights protect collective as well as individual rights and our most fundamental democratic right—to control our destiny through the election of our leadership—is clearly collective.

Perhaps the best way to understand the distinction between collective and individual rights is to ask not only who holds them, but *who might take them away?* The rights of individuals can be threatened by the majority, while the collective rights of that majority can be taken away by a tyrannical national government. Acting through the normal

Table 3.1 Collective Versus Individual Rights

	Who Holds	*Who Threatens*	*Who Protects*
Collective (Majoritarian)	the people (states)	national government (courts)	local majorities (legislatures)
Individual	individual citizens	local majorities (legislatures)	national government (courts)

mechanisms of representative government, majorities can impose on *individual* rights whether those are protections of free speech, religious observance, or against unreasonable searches. But the majority itself can lose *collective* rights when threatened by the national government. The ability of states or localities to decide their own destinies can be overturned by an aggressive or tyrannical power in Washington. This is the reason that the collective protections in the Bill of Rights are targeted toward the national government, including the ability to petition the federal government to redress grievances, to maintain a local militia to counterbalance federal power, and to insist upon local juries against federal prosecutions. While individual rights are protected best by federal courts, collective rights are protected best by state legislatures and local juries (see Table 3.1). The Constitution embodies both of these perspectives, although in the early days of the Republic the collective rights to self-determination were more prominent than the individual rights to resist the control of the majority.

The Fourteenth Amendment

This all leads to an important question: if the language of the Constitution discusses collective rights and the Founders had these in mind, why is it our assumption that the Constitution, especially the Bill of Rights, protects primarily individual rights? The answer lies in *the role of the Fourteenth Amendment*. In chapter 1 we discussed the convention of reading the Constitution *chronologically* (taking into account how later parts change earlier parts). The Amendment process is the core of a chronological reading and the Fourteenth Amendment is the most important agent of change. The central purpose of the Fourteenth Amendment was to alter the meaning of the entire Bill of Rights. Understanding this critical amendment is not only a matter of its language and intent, but also the history of how it was first ignored and then built upon in unexpected ways.

Most historians see the Civil War as the turning point when Americans shifted from regional allegiances to a national identity. In the way the American language was spoken prior to the war, the nation was a *plural* entity: Before the war the United States *were*; after the war the United States *was*. The Civil War Amendments (XIII, XIV, and XV) were designed to end the institution of slavery but also to unify the nation and the rights recognized throughout the union. The Fourteenth Amendment had the broader purpose of expanding liberties by applying all of the protections of the Bill of Rights against actions of state governments. Prior to this time, the Bill of Rights applied *only to the federal, but not local governments*. For example, the First Amendment's prohibition against "establishment of religion" (or government-sponsored congregations that could compel individuals to become members or pay tithes to support them) applied only to the federal government but not to the states. At the time of the founding of the nation, some states *did* have established churches, which were not prohibited by the Constitution. The early case of *Barron v. Baltimore* (1833), written by John Marshall, made clear that the Bill of Rights was only a federal and not a state matter. Hence when the First Amendment begins, "Congress shall make no law," it means exactly that, a restriction against the federal government alone. The original language of the Bill of Rights makes perfect sense when we remember that the Founders were more concerned with collective rights and the potential threat to those rights from the national government. State governments were much more free to regulate civic life as local majorities saw fit.

The Amendment would change this, applying the protections of the Bill of Rights against *all* levels of government. The specific language of the Fourteenth is "No state shall make or enforce any law which shall abridge the privileges or immunities of citizens of the United States." Interestingly, this does not have the common language meaning of applying the Bill of Rights in its entirety against the states or shifting collective rights to individual ones. In other words, one would not necessarily read that sentence and immediately understand its importance. Which led to the trouble. To make a long story short, during the political conflicts of Reconstruction following the Civil

War, many politicians and Justices were not in a mood to follow the broad meaning and goals of the Civil War Amendments. In a line of Supreme Court decisions beginning with the Slaughterhouse Cases in 1873, the Court ruled that the Privileges and Immunities Clause of the Fourteenth Amendment did not achieve its intended purpose. These rulings effectively delayed the application of the Bill of Rights to state laws until well into the twentieth century when the Court found novel ways of achieving the same ends.

Many have asked why the framers of the Fourteenth Amendment did not write in more clear language. Why did they not just say that the provisions of the first eight amendments now apply to all levels of government ("No state shall make or enforce any law which shall abridge the rights recognized in Amendments I through VIII")? The records of the debates in Congress suggest that the politicians of the time did not believe they would be misunderstood or could be willfully challenged. The phrase "privileges and immunities" is the basic legal definition of rights, which clearly include those of the Bill of Rights *but potentially others as well*. By using the broadest language possible, the framers intended to include not only the existing protections of the first eight amendments, but also any other rights that would be recognized in the future. This strategy of being universal rather than specific created the potential to be misunderstood and misappropriated.

The Fundamental Rights Doctrine

The history of the Fourteenth Amendment and its interpretation is crucial for understanding several landmark decisions on the meaning of the Constitution, because it led to an influential form of reasoning known as the *fundamental rights doctrine*. This interpretation has shaped countless modern decisions and is ingrained in the precedents. The broad acceptance of the doctrine masks that it is hard to justify without understanding that it is a means of achieving the broad purpose of the Fourteenth Amendment without doing so directly, which was not an option for the Court if it followed the precedent of the Slaughterhouse Cases and their aftermath. Some of the Justices, notably Hugo Black (on the bench from 1937 to 1971) and Clarence Thomas (1991 to the present), have argued that we should simply recognize now what the Privileges and Immunities Clause actually means. This idea is known as *total incorporation*: the Amendment incorporates (applies) all of the Bill of Rights to the actions of state and local governments. But this has been a minority opinion and another doctrine known as *selective incorporation* was followed in the twentieth-century history of the Court. This approach applied the provisions of the Bill of Rights against state governments piecemeal, one by one as appropriate cases came to the Court. Hence the broadening of individual protections in our system was slow and incremental, with some rights emerging before others.

Given this approach, the problem the Court had to solve was *How do you know if a given right should be incorporated?* The answer that emerged was that *fundamental rights* were incorporated, while rights that were deemed to be less than fundamental would not be enforced against the states. This sounds like an answer, but it begs another difficult question: *How do we know if a right is fundamental?* The Court developed the standard that fundamental rights are "so rooted in the traditions and conscience of our people as to be ranked as fundamental"; they are "implicit in the concept of ordered liberty" or "the very essence of a scheme of ordered liberty." These phrases come from the landmark cases of *Snyder v. Massachusetts* in 1934 and *Palko v. Connecticut* in 1937. We haven't discussed the phrase "ordered liberty" yet, but it refers to the goal of our constitutional system: a nation of liberty with stability, or the balance between individual rights and an orderly society upheld by majority rule. Without any right that is intrinsic to a scheme of ordered liberty, the constitutional system fails. Its absence would create a major break in the procedures and protections of a liberal democracy, such that the system is significantly damaged; the constitutional goal of balancing liberty and representation would fail in a meaningful way.

Following this definition, free speech is clearly fundamental. Without it we could not have the flow of information and debate necessary for meaningful elections that could allow us to control our representatives. The right of religious freedom is also fundamental, because without the ability to believe or worship as we choose, our basic liberty of thought is compromised. There is virtually no disagreement on those two points. Most observers agree with Justice Cardozo's position in the *Palko* decision that "neither liberty nor justice would exist if they were sacrificed." But other rights may or may not be fundamental in the same sense. It is worth noting that *Palko* established the fundamental rights doctrine in order to rule that a specific protection (double jeopardy in the case of an overturned conviction) was *not* a fundamental right that was enforced by the Fourteenth Amendment. One of the last provisions of the Bill of Rights to be recognized as fundamental was the Second Amendment right to bear arms, which was not addressed until 2010 in a controversial decision.

While the Court has gradually incorporated the enumerated rights of the Constitution, it has also expanded fundamental rights beyond those specifically mentioned in the document. The most controversial expansion is the right to privacy. The essence of *Roe v. Wade* is not merely the recognition of a privacy right that encompasses the choice to have an abortion, but the ruling that privacy is a *fundamental* right, which gives it the highest level of constitutional protection. This approach to rights and incorporation creates a potential conundrum. It means that some rights that are *not* mentioned specifically in the Constitution may be fundamental, such as privacy, while other rights that *are* enumerated in the document may *not* be fundamental. The most prominent example is the right to bear arms protected by the Second Amendment. Some contemporary thinkers believe that the circumstances of the nation have changed so much that a right designed to enable citizens to exert force against the power of the national government is no longer necessary to maintain a world of ordered liberty. Others argue that all fundamental rights remain fundamental; the appearance that any one of them is no longer necessary may only be the case because that bedrock freedom has been effective and hence its removal would put the system at risk.

The difference between enumerated rights that are *not* fundamental and non-enumerated rights that *are* fundamental illustrates the central criticism of this approach to understanding rights. The fundamental rights doctrine has greatly expanded the power of the Justices. Why? Because *they* get to decide what is fundamental and what is not. This decision determines how much protection a specific right has against government action. It is a decision controlled by the Court, through a doctrine that expands the discretion of the Justices rather than allowing the representative branches to have a greater say. Returning to our first point of conflict regarding judicial review, this explains the attitude toward the fundamental rights doctrine by those who believe judicial review should be limited versus those who believe it should be more expansive. The growth of the fundamental rights doctrine has increased the power of the Justices to decide important matters affecting American social policies rather than leaving such decisions to the peoples' representatives.

To summarize the complex history of the Fourteenth Amendment, it was intended to make all of the protections of the Bill of Rights apply to all levels of government, expanding the liberties enjoyed by American citizens. But the early decisions of the Supreme Court following its ratification refused to recognize this. Instead the Court employed a piecemeal method to bring in, or incorporate, specific provisions one by one. This created the concept of fundamental rights, which changed our understanding of the rights recognized or implied by the Constitution. The delay in the implementation of the Fourteenth Amendment resulted, ironically, in a greater expansion of rights beyond those clearly recognized in the document, through a doctrine open to greater interpretation.

Consequently, the fundamental rights doctrine and all of its implications are the product of an odd history rather than a clear reading of the Constitution. Yet in the minds of many legal thinkers, Justices, and academics, we are shackled to it because it is enshrined in the precedents, regardless of whether we would go down that path if we were to begin from the beginning. The fundamental rights doctrine also accomplishes something aside from redeeming the original goal of the Fourteenth Amendment: it expands the power of the Supreme Court, especially if the Justices wish to find rights outside of the text of the document. The early misreading of the Fourteenth Amendment and the subsequent rise of the fundamental rights doctrine led to either important achievements or acts of mischief depending on one's perspective.

The Implications of Collective Versus Individual Rights

For our purposes of understanding this point of conflict, the heart of the issue is the distinction between the early vision of collective rights that empower majorities to act and the later vision of individual rights that protect us from that same majority. The Fourteenth Amendment added an individual focus to the collective bent of the original document. The controversy is whether it eradicated those collective rights in favor of individual ones or simply added individual rights to the mix, leaving a broad scope for majoritarian rights. *Have rights become fully individual to the point that they trump the ability of local majorities to determine their own practices, regulations, or morals?* With this divisive question in mind, we can turn to two other points of conflict: *federalism*, or the independent powers of states balanced against the national government, and *ordered liberty*, or the balance between individual freedoms and the goal of a decent society that enforces limits to disruptive behavior. These two concepts are distinct but reinforce each other. The next two chapters focus on these conflicts, but we will not stray far from the central concept of rights, especially the questions of who holds them and who may threaten to take them away.

4

FEDERALISM

Must We Have One National Standard?

The central goal of the Constitution can be phrased as either empowering democracy or avoiding tyranny; it depends on whether you want to focus on achieving the positive or avoiding the negative. Almost any paragraph or principle of the document is aimed toward one or both of these goals. Federalism is about employing geography to avoid tyranny, as well as localizing government to empower democratic majorities.

Many of the Founders believed that the inevitable corruption of any political power was connected directly to geography; simply put, the greater the number of different geographic divisions with separate governments, the less likely it is that any one of them will take over. Federalism is the idea that the authority to make decisions must be divided among the national and state governments in order to avoid the concentration of power. Unchecked power at the federal level could lead to a loss of democratic control and the slow slide toward the destruction of collective and individual liberty. The longer the constitutional order survives, the less the fear of tyranny resonates with many citizens, which explains a great deal of the contemporary conflict. Our current debate is whether the principle of federalism still holds sway or whether the changes that have occurred in our nation have made it less important than other vital concerns.

Divided government is a clear feature of the Constitution. The Congress, the president, and the Supreme Court are set at odds intentionally, trading away the likelihood of efficient government for protection against a tyrannical one. This can be thought of as a horizontal division of government among the three branches, but the system was also designed to have a vertical division grounded in geographical separation. The national government has only limited powers relating to the governance of the country as a whole, while the state governments have control over most of the affairs within their own jurisdictions. When many local governments jealously guard their own prerogatives, this ensures that the federal government does not intrude too much into the lives of citizens. In this sense, federalism is a reflection of the broader principle of divided government.

This suggests that states matter for preserving liberties, but also that they matter in preserving local cultures. Different parts of a continental nation may have different values or traditions that they want to maintain. We may want to allow diversity rather than insist on one national standard. Simply put, do Massachusetts and Texas need to be the same? Must we insist that the way things are done in New Hampshire is the same way they are done in New Mexico? Regions with a long-standing identity may want to maintain it, and people with different values may want to be able to choose the culture of the coasts or the culture of the interior. On the other hand, individuals who travel to different places in the union may want their rights to move with them. In a nation of individual rights with a mobile population (especially among middle-class professionals who often relocate because of their career), regional differences may need to take a back seat to individual rights. Does our nation need to have one standard for values, procedures, and rights, or can it have a meaningful diversity guided by the democratic process in each region? *The first justification of federalism is avoiding tyranny. The second justification is regional difference.* The current dispute is whether it remains an important principle given the changes that have taken place in our nation as well as the amendments that have been made to the Constitution.

Where Is Federalism in the Constitution?

Federalism is both a specific and a general principle of the Constitution, meaning that it is found in the text and in the structure of the document. The primary textual location is the Tenth Amendment. The Ninth and Tenth are unlike the first eight amendments in the sense that they do not discuss specific protections, but instead express broad understandings of rights. When read together, they explain the relationships among the federal government, the state governments, and the American people:

> *Amendment IX:* The enumeration in the Constitution, of certain rights, shall not be construed to deny or disparage others retained by the people.
>
> *Amendment X:* The powers not delegated to the United States by the Constitution, nor prohibited by it to the states, are reserved to the states respectively, or to the people.

The Ninth Amendment says that there are rights aside from the specific ones described in the Constitution. The holders of those rights are the American people, both collectively and individually. The exact nature of those rights is not made clear, which creates a source of continuing controversy. The Tenth Amendment addresses the distribution of government powers rather than of individual rights. All powers not given to the national government are reserved to the state governments, unless specifically prohibited. It is not that the states have specific powers and the remainder falls into the federal realm, but the reverse. The national government has the specific powers mentioned, while the bulk of normal governance takes place at the state level.

The Ninth and Tenth Amendments are easier to understand when considered together, because they address both kinds of constitutional restraint on government: limited powers of our representatives to act in the first place and boundaries to what the government can do to individuals when it does act. The first are *structural limits* and the second are *rights-based limits*. The Tenth Amendment deals with structure (specific powers go to the national level and general power to the state level), while the Ninth deals with rights (the Constitution recognizes specific ones but endorses others held by states and individuals). That is the essence of federalism.

But the principle is not merely in the specific language of the Bill of Rights. Even without those amendments, the Constitution would still be essentially a Federalist document because the system it creates is one of divided and separated regional powers. The Senate is designed on the Federalist principle, with two senators from each state regardless of the population. Less than a million people live in some of the less populous states like North Dakota, Delaware, or Vermont, while over 37 million live in California. A senator from Wyoming represents around 300,000 citizens, while a senator from Texas represents over 12 million. The selection of the president through the Electoral College rather than by a national popular vote achieves the same purpose of representing states rather than individuals.

Beyond the way representation is allocated by geography, the central facet of the Constitution that reflects federalism is how powers are distributed. The powers granted to the primary national institution—the Congress—are specific and limited. Article I begins by describing how members of Congress will be elected and organized (Sections 1 through 6). Section 7 gives the House of Representatives the sole power of raising federal revenue. Section 8 describes the specific powers of Congress, while Section 9 details what it *cannot* do. There is no broad or general grant of power to the national legislature, but only a list of specific ones. They begin with the "power to lay and collect taxes," "To borrow money," etc., and end with the broadest statement, known as the Necessary and Proper Clause: "To make all laws which shall be necessary and proper for carrying into execution the foregoing powers, and all other powers vested by this Constitution in the government of the United States." But only those powers. As Lincoln phrased it in his First Inaugural Address, "By the frame of the government under which we live, this same people have wisely given their public servants but little power for mischief."[15]

While the Constitution speaks of explicit and limited powers of the national government, individual states remain essentially unencumbered, free to run their own domains as they see fit as long as they do not violate specific provisions of the Constitution. Even elections laws for national offices remain under state control: "The times, places and manner of holding elections for Senators and Representatives, shall be prescribed in each state by the legislature thereof." The only specific limits on a state's power to govern are found in Articles IV and VI, including their obligation to give "full faith and credit" to the legal proceedings of other states, to extradite persons charged with a crime in another state, to avoid any religious test for holding public office, and to maintain "a republican form of government." The meaning of this last phrase is not clear, but it suggests at minimum a system in which government officials are accountable through elections. Aside from this general idea, states are left mostly alone.

Challenges to Federalism

If federalism is found in these aspects of the Constitution, why do some say it is not an important principle? The question is not whether it *was* there, but instead whether it is *still* there. Opponents of federalism argue that it is has been lessened or eliminated by subsequent changes. Those new developments came in two forms: cultural changes to the nation and structural changes to the Constitution. The most important cultural change was the nationalization of our self-perception as well as our economy. Once upon a time, most Americans thought of themselves more as citizens of their state than as citizens of the United States, but this is no longer true. Instead we have national institutions, national media, a national military, and for most citizens a fully national sense of self. Citizens travel and live in various parts of the country during the course of their lives in a manner unheard of at the time the nation was founded. This shift to a national rather than regional focus is not merely a matter of changed attitudes, but also a question of how this change interacts with different aspects of the constitutional order.

As a justification for federal action, the power of Congress cited most often is also the most controversial: the Interstate Commerce Clause, which grants to Congress the ability to "regulate commerce with foreign nations, and among the several states." This appears to say that Congress can regulate commerce that deals with *national* trade, which occurs "among the several states." This fits with the division of labor described in the Tenth Amendment: explicit powers that apply to the whole union fall to the federal government, while general powers dealing with purely local matters are reserved to various state governments. The grant of power for *interstate* trade seems to suggest that Congress does not have broader power over trade that does not cross state lines or occurs solely within a local area. Most regulation of commerce and other activity falls under what is called the *police power*. This does not refer to literal law enforcement by police, but to any regulating of society, from speed limits to housing codes to vaccination requirements. The traditional common law definition of the police power is the ability to regulate society for the safety, health, and morality of the population. In a Federalist system, only state governments have the police power, while the federal government explicitly does not.

So how much power does the ability to regulate interstate commerce create for the Congress? The answer depends on what is considered *commerce* and what is considered to be *interstate*. In the early days of the nation, little trade was conducted across state lines. Compared to what we see today, there was very little commerce at all. But in this century most of what we buy is manufactured in one part of the country before being shipped across state lines to where it is purchased. As the nation has grown in the last two hundred years, the scope of economic activity has magnified tremendously. And as we became a more commercial nation, the power of Congress has grown as well. The controversial question is how far this power extends.

The second challenge to federalism is not about gradual changes to the nation, but dramatic changes to the Constitution itself. When the Fourteenth Amendment altered the nature of rights, making them more individual and enforcing their protection against state governments, it also may have altered the relationship between the national and state governments. Earlier we discussed the distinction between structural limits on whether government is empowered to act and rights-based limits on how far government can go; the first creates boundaries to even starting a government action, while the second recognizes limits on what that action can influence. The Fourteenth Amendment increased the rights-based limits to government. About that there is no disagreement. But what did that change mean for the previous structural limits inherent in federalism? There are three ways that the Fourteenth Amendment may have reduced or eliminated the structural limits on the federal government, effectively writing federalism out of the document.

1. It changed our system to one of rights protections. After the Fourteenth, the primary check on federal government power is no longer that it can't act at all, but that it can't act in ways that encroach on expansive individual rights. Therefore structural limits are unnecessary.
2. It made all levels of government operate on the same principles. Regardless of whether the roles of state and federal governments were intended to be different prior to the Fourteenth Amendment, afterward they are now the same. If federal and state governments are the same, structural limits on federal action are no longer in force.

3. It increased the power of the federal government. Less power at the state level necessitates greater power at the national level in order to keep the system in balance and provide for the level of governance we need. This last idea illustrates two very different interpretations of what the Fourteenth Amendment accomplished. The first is that it lessened the power of states while federal power remained the same, resulting in greater total freedom for our citizens. The second is that it lessened the power of states and, because the total amount of government power must be kept in equilibrium, it therefore increased the power of the federal government. Readers of the Constitution disagree about whether it is self-adjusting in order to maintain the original level of power even if redistributed or whether the amendment process can alter the total amount of government power.

When we combine these three possible effects of the Fourteenth Amendment with the cultural and economic changes that have taken place on a national scale, the principle of federalism is in retreat from its previous status. It may or may not still be a vital principle at the core of the Constitution. Much of this depends on our premise about the regional or national nature of America. We have experienced increasing unity since the Civil War, but may have been experiencing increasing divisions in the last decades of culture wars since the 1970s. The unresolved question is to what degree we have distinct regions or divisions in our nation compared to one unified culture. This leads to what some commentators call "moral federalism," or the idea that we have different value systems in coastal and interior America, which do not easily mix, especially on questions of abortion, gay marriage, public religiosity, and other value-laden political issues. Either there is a necessity for moral agreement within the nation or it is reasonable to have prevailing moral differences in distinct regions of a large republic.

Where Is Federalism Now?

If there is a continuum from a core principle to a dead principle of the Constitution, the question is *Where does federalism fall on this dimension?* While one group believes the principle is a vital part of our system, another group disagrees. Some find federalism in the Tenth Amendment and the structure of the Constitution, as well as in the writings and beliefs of the Founders. Another group cares less about the Founders' preoccupations than about contemporary concerns grounded in a national culture. They do not see federalism in the structure of the post-Fourteenth Amendment Constitution and view the Tenth Amendment as an anachronism in a unified nation. The first camp says that it is not possible to eradicate a constitutional principle through cultural change. That is possible only by amendment, and the Fourteenth doesn't do that. It expanded liberty by increasing the role of individual rights and reducing the power of state governments, but it did not *increase* federal power. Federalism, therefore, remains a vital part of the constitutional order. The second camp argues that the Fourteenth Amendment and the major changes in our national culture and economy have made federalism a lesser doctrine or eliminated it altogether.

One's perspective on federalism is connected to the other points of conflict in clear ways. If rights are collective, then federalism is an important means of protecting the power of state and local governments. If rights are individualized, then federalism is subordinate to personal liberty. The ability of states to decide their own standards for moral issues like gay marriage and abortion relies upon the Federalist principle, while the rejection of federalism increases the claim to uniform rights throughout the union. Aside from moral questions, conflicts over the legalization of marijuana, the enforcement of illegal immigration laws, and even the application of national health care laws revolve around local challenges to national standards. Also closely tied to federalism is a long-standing debate over the nature of liberty and the extent of the police power. The next chapter discusses this vital point of conflict between competing conceptions of constitutional liberty.

5

LIBERTY

Does the Constitution Invoke *Ordered Liberty* or *Pure Liberty*?

The heart of constitutional conflict is majority rule versus individual rights. Both are core principles of our system, but they are in inevitable conflict. Majority rule ensures that our citizens can control the government rather than the reverse. The Founders didn't want rule by the mob any more than they wanted a monarchy, but the majority gets its way in an orderly fashion through representation (a republic) even if we do not put every decision to a direct vote of the people (a true democracy). At the heart of the system, the people have the final say in determining our destiny. The second core principle is individual rights, which limit how far the majority can go in controlling citizens. Specific liberties of speech, religion, and bearing arms, along with broad protections against arbitrary searches and improper criminal prosecutions, are all aimed specifically against the actions of the majority. Both the control of government through majority rule and the preservation of human dignity through individual rights sound excellent to us, so it is easy to forget that they are contradictory. They mean that the majority can rule, except when it can't. The people can enact their preferences, except when they aren't allowed to do so. In short, the system makes no sense to a casual observer. The continual question of American constitutional politics is *What balance can we find between our two core principles?*

Ordered Liberty

One traditional answer to this search for balance is the principle of *ordered liberty*. It was the Founders' vision of the best and most workable standard for a society that upholds both democracy and rights.

But it no longer holds sway against a growing challenge from a newer and broader vision of what could be called *pure liberty*. Neither phrase appears in the Constitution, but the concept of ordered liberty suffuses the writings of the founding generation. The term is frequently attributed to George Washington himself, although there is doubt about whether he ever used the exact phrase. There is no doubt, however, that he believed the concept was a cornerstone of our constitutional system.

Ordered liberty means liberty without license. Another way of phrasing this is freedom with decency. If we had no worries about the nature of humans or the fragility of society, liberty in and of itself would be our sole concern, or as James Madison phrased it in *Federalist 51*, "If men were angels, no government would be necessary." However, the situation is more complex if we want liberty but know that people are problematic. We want a decent world as well as a free one, a world in which we can raise children and have a sense of security for our families. To achieve this we must have *ordered* liberty, or the proper balance between individual freedoms and personal responsibilities.

It may sound contradictory to discuss liberty and its limits in the same breath, but the Founders believed that *rights and responsibilities were inseparable.* That is what made the system work. Individuals were free to live their own lives, but were also expected to act decently and contribute to the defense of the system. The primary responsibility of able-bodied males was to defend society against threats, which is why all were members of the militia, the inactive military body that organized when things went south. The Founders' vision of intertwined liberties and responsibilities has been mostly abandoned in the contemporary world, but the resonance of that idea remains.

The distinction between *free* and *unfree* does not imply that there is no distinction between *appropriate* and *inappropriate*. Free and irresponsible are not synonymous. This is the case because liberty is not merely an end in itself. Freedom for its own sake is not necessarily valuable and often leads to results that are exactly the opposite. Liberty has a different cast if we see it as having the higher purpose of not just a free but also a decent life, which includes security, decorum, and civilized norms. Another way to phrase this is just because you *can* do something does not mean you *should* do it. Decent restraint is as much a part of a free society as liberty.

Ordered liberty is perhaps best defined as *balance*. Often there are two evils that we want to avoid and veering too far to either side is our downfall. This kind of thinking can be described as seeking a *golden mean*, an idea we took from Greek philosophy. The intuition is that vices are found at the extremes and virtue in the middle. Any virtue taken to the extreme becomes a vice. This is true even of our greatest virtues, like love and charity, or even minor ones like caution. If we love someone too much, we become fawning, obsessive, and ignore other people. It is unhealthy and leads to a bad end. If we take charity too far, we give away everything and leave nothing for ourselves, becoming paupers who can give nothing. Caution is an important virtue, but too much leads to never leaving your house. In politics, the vices of the extremes are even more clear: being too aggressive toward other nations versus being too weak and inviting attack; having too few police versus too many; too little concern for the poor versus creating incentives for people to not work. The tension that may matter most in a democratic society is the choice between too little freedom and too much: the twin evils of tyranny and anarchy, the king and the mob. This is illustrated by the excesses of the French Revolution, which was inspired by our Revolution but then degraded into mob violence. Too little liberty and the king is putting people in prison; too much license and the mob is cutting off people's heads. The best path is the middle ground. This was the heart of the Founders' view of politics: a free government must avoid the opposing extremes of tyranny and disorder.

Pure Liberty

Edmund Burke—the British statesman and philosopher who supported the American cause but reviled the French Revolution for its excesses—famously wrote that "liberty must be limited in order to be possessed," for "what is liberty without wisdom, and without virtue? It is the greatest of all possible evils; for it is folly, vice, and madness, without tuition or restraint. Those who know what virtuous liberty is, cannot bear to see it disgraced by incapable heads, on account of their having high-sounding words in their mouths."[16] The high-sounding words in defense of a broader vision of individual liberty began to have much more impact in the 1800s, after Burke was no longer around to ridicule them. Perhaps the most famous argument was made by John Stuart Mill in *On Liberty*, published in 1859. This influential pamphlet defines liberty as the right to do as one wishes until it causes literal harm to someone else. As Assistant District Attorney Jack McCoy phrased it on *Law & Order* (which can provide a great deal of legal knowledge if you watch enough episodes), "your right to throw a punch stops at someone else's face." A citizen can do whatever they want as long as it does not cause direct harm to others. This does not include *indirect* harm, which enters the realm of moral injuries. However, many Americans are concerned about public morality, especially as it affects their kids. Maybe public displays of profane language or sexual behavior *do* cause harm. For example, we have nudity laws for a reason. Streaking in college is a time-honored tradition more humorous than harmful, but twenty years later when someone drops trou in front of your children you may not have the same reaction. The boundary of harm is not so easy to discern in some cases, but the *On Liberty* standard limits it to direct, clear damage. Paternalism is also not a sufficient excuse to interfere with the choices of adults, even if they are poor choices that may cause foreseeable harm, like smoking crystal meth or engaging in prostitution, both of which seem like better ideas in the beginning than a few years later.

The pertinent question is whether indirect harms are taken seriously. The pure liberty perspective argues that they are minor compared to the more important claims of individual freedom. This is especially the case when the alleged harms can be avoided by simply looking away. Perhaps the feeling of harm is often the result of intolerance. From the perspective of ordered liberty, individual actions may damage our collective liberties, or the ability of the majority to create a decent world that protects their interests. Therefore the majority can impose limits on individual actions in the name of decency and encourage individual citizens to live up to their duties. The traditional definition of the police power (which is held by local communities and state governments) was the ability to regulate behavior in the interests of the *safety*, *health*, and *morality* of the community. The emerging conception of pure liberty argues that regulation for the sake of morality is no longer legitimate.

The idea of pure liberty—or a liberty not associated with responsibilities—was a nineteenth-century development, which seems natural to us in the twenty-first century, but was quite new at that time. It would have seemed bizarre to most Americans in the early days of the nation, but it has become mainstream now to the point that Mill is cited frequently as a basic definition of liberty in the current culture. His view is even sometimes invoked as a *conservative* definition because it does require *some* limits, disallowing some behavior, which is more restrictive than a growing group of contemporary thinkers believe is warranted. Mill's pure liberty is the opposite of Burke's "manly, moral, regulated liberty."[17] While self-restraint and a regard for others are at the heart of ordered liberty, they have no necessary place in a system of pure liberty. This leads to inevitable litigation.

Bong Hits Revisited

We began our discussion of reading the Constitution with the Bong Hits case and we are far from finished with Joseph Frederick and his antagonist Deborah Morse, the high school principal who attempted to uphold the educational mission of the people of Alaska against his questionable conduct. In the previous discussion of *Morse v. Frederick*, we concentrated on its premise aspect. But the case is not only about whether students hold the same rights as adults. It is also about whether pure liberty is the new standard. Under the traditional understanding of ordered liberty, local authorities have broad discretion to maintain public decency. This includes public displays that the community finds objectionable. When public schools are involved the discretion granted by the ordered liberty standard is even broader because the community has a strong interest in the safety, health, and morality with which kids are taught. The role of schools and minors in *Morse* illustrates the interconnection of premises and principles, which are not entirely distinct but instead influence each other in subtle ways. The premise that minors are meaningfully different from adults tilts the argument toward ordered liberty as a means of protecting and teaching them. On the other hand, if they are the same as adults, then they need no special protections and pure liberty can apply. The Court's decision about the nature of students led to the implicit ruling that ordered liberty is still the prevailing standard in regard to public schools.

The recent case that deals most directly with the debate over the nature of liberty is *Phelps*. You recall the facts of the Phelps case from the introduction: the Westboro Baptist Church picketed the funeral of a fallen Marine, whose father sued for what is called intentional infliction of emotional distress. This kind of claim requires a high burden of proof that the defendant's conduct was extreme and outrageous, causing severe emotional damage. The jury found that these standards had been met and awarded a rare victory to the plaintiff. However, the Supreme Court ruled that the First Amendment protects Phelps against all liability, given that his speech was political in nature. Even though private individuals were involved, the topic was of public concern (homosexuality and the Iraq War). The ruling represents a major change in free speech doctrine, which used to require courts to consider "the totality of the circumstances" to determine if speech is outside of the bounds of the First Amendment's protection. The "time, place, and manner," or "content, form, and context" of the communication were all taken into consideration. But *Phelps* indicates a new approach: political content alone invokes the full protection of the Constitution, regardless of the rest of the circumstances; content now trumps context. All political speech is protected from all liability.

Even more than broadening the freedom of speech, the Court is invoking pure liberty and rejecting ordered liberty as the appropriate standard. How you react to the *Phelps* ruling may be a good measure of your view of this conflict. The Court's ruling established a new standard, that not only is any sort of political expression free from government restriction, but the speaker is also free from responsibility for any harm the speech may cause. There is no legal recourse available against bad behavior, even in the most delicate personal circumstances such as a funeral; the community has no means of protection against its mean-spirited or anti-social members. In other words, the ruling means that the principle of ordered liberty is dying in regard to free speech, being replaced by pure liberty as the constitutional standard.

6

RELIGION

Is the Constitution a Religious or Secular Document?

The Declaration of Independence begins by invoking "the Laws of Nature and of Nature's God," refers to our "Creator" and "the Supreme Judge of the world," and ends with a "firm reliance of the protection of Divine Providence." The Constitution, however, makes very little reference to God. Is this a distinct change from the religious worldview of the Declaration, or was that worldview simply assumed? What does it mean if we see the Constitution as having largely secular or meaningfully religious foundations? The ramifications begin with the conflicts over the place of religion in public life. If it is a foundation of the system, this provides support for government recognition of religion. It justifies the Court's position in *Zorach v. Clauson* in 1952 that "We are a religious people whose institutions presuppose a Supreme Being." On the other hand, a system designed to reflect the increasingly secular nature of the American people leads in a very different direction. This justifies the Court's position in *Lemon v. Kurtzman* in 1971 that the government must not entangle itself with religion, disallowing any "intimate and continuing relationship between church and state."

But the larger implications center on the nature of rights. In chapter 3 we discussed the conflict over whether constitutional rights are individual or collective. This is one of two central questions that divide our understanding of rights. The first was *Who holds them (individuals or groups)?* The second is *Where do they come from?* We can agree about who has a right but disagree about why, or how they got it. The problem facing contemporary readers of the Constitution is whether to follow the understanding of rights as they were perceived when the nation was founded or to understand rights as many in our society see them today. The Founders saw rights as being granted by God and intertwined with responsibilities (especially rights to personal free-dom, creating the standard of ordered liberty discussed earlier). Many contemporary thinkers see rights as purely secular ideas granted by society and held by all citizens regardless of their actions. The God-given rights of the Founders are immutable and everlasting, while the socially constructed rights of contemporary secular thinkers are mal-leable and open to expansion or contraction. Our current dilemma is that our society has not abandoned one view for the other; we have many religious citizens just as we have many secular ones (and the divide between the two groups seems to be growing), which makes this a contentious point of conflict. It extends well beyond questions of religion in the public square to shape other aspects of constitutional interpretation: *What is the nature of rights?* (Do they pre-date the Constitution or were they created by the Constitution?) and *How open are rights to change?* (Do they protect us from attempts to alter them or are they open to alteration as society evolves?) The question of whether the Constitution is at heart a religious or secular document is more influential than at first it seems. Perhaps the most clear place to begin is with the parts of the Constitution that address religion directly.

The Dual Religion Clauses

The first concern of the First Amendment is religion. It offers two dif-ferent perspectives on the relationship between God and the govern-ment, ideas that are generally invoked separately but make more sense when read together.

> *Amendment I*:   Congress shall make no law *respecting an estab-lishment of religion*, or *prohibiting the free exercise thereof*; or abridging the freedom of speech, or of the press; or the right of the people peaceably to assemble, and to petition the gov-ernment for a redress of grievances.

How are we to make sense of these two opening clauses? The phrase often suggested is the "separation of church and state," which many Americans believe is in the Constitution. It isn't. It was coined by Thomas Jefferson, who considered one of his greatest accomplishments to be writing the Statute for Religious Freedom for his home state of Virginia. The phrase is closer in meaning to the Establishment Clause, which seems to limit religion, but further away from the Free Exercise

Clause that seems to empower it. A common inference from Jefferson's phrase is that our government is to be fully secular, with religion having no connection to public life; in this view the goal of a "wall of separation" was to create a secular society. But this interpretation is both an expansion of Jefferson's influence and a bastardization of his views. While often cited as a representative of the Founding generation, Jefferson was one of the more secular Founders. Rather than take Jefferson as representative, we may as well take Washington, who was openly devout and certain of the necessity of religion for the preservation of the union. Jefferson was a leading voice of the early days of the Revolution and the writing of the Declaration, but was not a major influence during the post-Revolution period, including the writing of the Constitution. (He was in France during the drafting and ratification debates.) Moreover, Jefferson agreed with the predominance of Founders that a religious society was a benefit to free government. The *relatively* secular Jefferson drafted a Declaration of Independence that is clearly religious, referencing God at least four times. What is really being said in the contemporary view is that *we* have become more secular in recent times, not that the Founders or their understanding of our system was secular.

The common language meaning of the dual clauses suggests something else. The first clause says what government *cannot* do; the second what citizens *can* do. Together they provide a set of boundaries for a free and religious society: the government can't make you uphold a specific religion and you can practice the religion of your choosing. If read alone, the first seems to restrict religion while the second expands it. But what they do together is say that religion is free from interference. The purpose of the establishment clause in the minds of the Framers was not to create a secular world, but quite the contrary, *to protect religion from government intervention so that religion would flourish.* Religion is free from government as much as government is free from religion. Perhaps it is more accurate to say that government is free from religious denominations or religious practice, but not from the concepts or ramifications of Christian thought, which framed the original understanding of rights.

Unalienable Rights and Their Origins

The Declaration of Independence invokes *unalienable rights.* We know that "among these are Life, Liberty and the pursuit of Happiness," but we may no longer know what it means to be *unalienable*. Many people assume this term refers to a right that cannot be taken from us. But this is not complete. An unalienable right is one that is so much a part of what it means to be a free-standing human that *even we* cannot alienate ourselves from it. The point is not that it cannot be taken away, but instead that it *cannot be given away*, a much stronger statement. This is why it is impermissible to sell ourselves into slavery, even if we believed we wanted to.

In the worldview of the Founders, not only were certain core rights unalienable, but also certain responsibilities. Rights and responsibilities were intertwined in such a strong fashion that one did not make much sense without the other. These ideas have faded in our contemporary culture. We now tend to see rights as free-floating and responsibilities as limited, but it is important to recognize this change.[18]

Unalienable rights are distinguished not only in how they operate, but also in how they originated. In the worldview of the Founders, rights are unalienable because they were granted by God. Why are we free? Because we were imbued by God with free will. Why is equality a core value? Because we are all equal in the eyes of God. This is the essential argument of the *natural law* or *natural rights* tradition, which sees rights as God-given (natural), and therefore independent and prior to any arrangement made by man. One of our most important statements about the nature of rights is at the heart of the Declaration of Independence:

> **We hold these truths to be self-evident, that all men are created equal, that they are endowed by their Creator with certain unalienable** Rights, that among these are Life, Liberty and the pursuit of Happiness. — **That to secure these rights, Governments are instituted among Men**

These forty-seven words say several vital things: rights come from God; they are unalienable; an essential equality among men derives from the same source; liberty is a central right; and the role of government is not to create rights, but to protect those that already exist. After invoking unalienable rights, the Declaration states, "That to secure these rights, Governments are instituted among Men." The Constitution embodies this theory of natural rights by raising protections *against* government, which is not the source of rights but instead is a potential danger to them.

The natural law orientation is reflected in the language of the Bill of Rights. Each amendment either identifies certain acts that the government will not do or identifies a right that will be maintained. The language never creates, establishes, grants, or otherwise originates a right. For example, the First Amendment states that Congress shall make no law "abridging the freedom of speech." It could have said that it endows citizens with a right to free speech, but it does not. The right preceded the Constitution, which merely vows to protect it. Similarly, the Second Amendment states that the right to bear arms "shall not be infringed," also implying that it already existed. The other amendments recognize rights that "shall not be violated," or "shall be preserved." The Constitution does not establish rights, but only establishes a government that protects rights; it is not a mechanism for creation, but for preservation of what was given by God. From the contemporary perspective, this was a nice gift, but we would have gotten there through reason anyway. The Constitution itself was an act of collective intellect, and has over time become its own source of rights regardless of the prevalent beliefs at the time it was written. The contentious question is what the religious origins mean for politics in a more secular society. If our rights are natural ones, this presents a problem in the contemporary world. We have created a secular society, in which religion is no longer the dominant justification for our beliefs or actions. If rights are God-given, but we have killed God (as Nietzsche famously phrased it), do we still have our rights? This is no small problem for a secular society.

The alternative position is that rights derive from the people. We have the rights that we have asserted, fought for, and collectively protect. We have the rights that we mutually accord one another. In this sense, rights are created rather than eternal, which means that new rights can emerge as society evolves. In this view, the Constitution itself is a source of rights, as an organic creation of our people. However, if rights come from the people, the people can take them back. Created rights are alterable in the same way they emerged, which places our rights in a less protected framework.

A third perspective on the origin of rights comes from traditional conservatism—that we have the rights that have been handed down from our culture and history. The source of rights is tradition rather than God or cultural evolution. Many of the revolutionaries of the Founding Era argued that the British Crown had infringed upon their ancient rights, which they traced to the heritage of English yeomen from the time of Magna Carta on the field at Runnymede in 1215, when the British nobles forced King John to recognize limits to his power. Similar to the constructed rights perspective, traditional rights were created by man rather than God, only so long ago that they feel eternal. Similar to the natural rights perspective, traditional rights are stronger and do not change, as opposed to the constructed rights view in which rights are open to growth but also to destruction.

So, are rights *from God, from the people*, or *from tradition*? If they are from God, they are more stable, but may mean little in a secular world. If they are from the people, they can be altered by the same people who created them, with little protection from the will of the majority. If they are from tradition, they are stable, but limited to those that have existed in the past. In either the first or last conception of rights, they pre-date the Constitution, which acts as a guardian rather than a source of rights. In the social view, the Constitution itself is a source of rights, but not the only one in a continually evolving society. God-given or traditional rights pre-date the Constitution and are not amenable to change or evolution, while socially endowed rights are more flexible and expansive. The first kind of rights are limited in number but are stronger, while the second kind are potentially broader but weaker.

A final ramification of the religious versus secular distinction is how it relates to other points of conflict, specifically the support or opposition it lends to ordered liberty. If morality is a necessary bulwark to a free society, then local communities are more empowered to uphold appropriate standards of behavior, especially in encouraging decency within schools and other public institutions. President Eisenhower once famously phrased this argument that "our form of government makes no sense unless it is founded in a deeply felt religious faith, and I don't care what it is." The specific Judeo-Christian tradition was not relevant as long as one was present. This raises the question of the degree to which as a nation we really have moved (or can move) away from our religious roots. In other words, is *Zorach* still correct in its assertion that we are a religious people? This is a far-reaching point of conflict that subtly shapes our perspective on the Constitution.

7

TRANSCENDENCE

Do Transcendent Rights Exist in the Constitution?

One of the most neglected parts of the Constitution is the sentence that provides its justification. Many of us can quote the Preamble (especially if singing counts, from the Schoolhouse Rock! television spots),[19] but it is cited only rarely in decisions of the Supreme Court. It is one long sentence, with many qualifiers:

> We the people of the United States, in order to form a more perfect union, establish justice, insure domestic tranquility, provide for the common defense, promote the general welfare, and secure the blessings of liberty to ourselves and our posterity, do ordain and establish this Constitution for the United States of America.

The stated purposes of the Constitution include national unity, good government in the sense of justice, tranquility, defense, or general welfare, and last but not least the protection of liberty. Securing freedom in its many aspects seems to be one of the primary goals of the document. That was the claim of Henning Jacobson, who argued in 1902 that mandatory vaccination laws infringed on his individual liberty to decide matters of personal health and control over his own body. Therefore they violated the Preamble and were "opposed to the spirit of the Constitution."[20] The Supreme Court disagreed in *Jacobson v. Massachusetts*, ruling that "[a]lthough the preamble indicates the general purposes for which the people ordained and established the Constitution, it has never been regarded as the source of any substantive power conferred on the government of the United States."[21] This may be misconstruing Jacobson's claim, which was not that the

Preamble granted substantive powers *to* the government, but that it precluded powers *from* it, limiting them to those in accord with the Preamble.

Perhaps more importantly, the Court rejected Jacobson's broader argument:

> We also pass without discussion the suggestion that the above section of the statute is opposed to the spirit of the Constitution. Undoubtedly, as observed by Chief Justice Marshall, speaking for the court in *Sturges v. Crowninshield* ... "the spirit of an instrument, especially of a constitution, is to be respected not less than its letter; yet the spirit is to be collected chiefly from its words." We have no need in this case to go beyond the plain, obvious meaning of the words in those provisions of the Constitution.[22]

Before and since *Jacobson* the Court has almost never cited the Preamble, but it has moved closer over time to the position that the Constitution contains broad values that can limit government. Whether Jacobson had a point—not about vaccination laws, but about the broader purposes or themes of the Constitution—is one of the most divisive conflicts in reading the Constitution.

This concept can be described as *transcendence*: the perspective that the Constitution invokes broad principles that rise above any specific provision. The question is whether the Constitution is a document of clear instructions for governance or a document of grand ideas. If it is more than the sum of its parts, then we can discern its overall meaning and employ these transcendent values to decide constitutional controversies. On the other hand, if it is a specific charter for governance, then we should pay attention to precisely what it says. The heart of the issue is the convention of reading the Constitution *comprehensively*. Reading a specific clause or section for its exact meaning is one thing, but reading the whole document for its broader ideas can lead to much more problematic conclusions, which is why this is the most controversial of the four conventions. In law school, most often the Constitution is examined clause by clause, sometimes with specific classes devoted to just one amendment or section. If it is read comprehensively, it can take on a different meaning. Alexander Bickel, the conservative legal scholar we mentioned earlier, called this the Constitution's "hospitality to large purposes."[23] The Supreme Court in 1947 called them the Constitution's "majestic generalities."[24] In *Poe v. Ullman* in 1961 Justice John Marshall Harlan argued in his dissent that we should read the Constitution "not in a literalistic way, as if we had a tax statute before us, but as the basic charter of our society, setting out in spare but meaningful terms the principles of government." In his view, liberty "is not a series of isolated points pricked out in terms of the taking of property; the freedom of speech, press, and religion; the right to keep and bear arms; the freedom from unreasonable searches and seizures; and so on. It is a rational continuum which, broadly speaking, includes a freedom from all substantial arbitrary impositions and purposeless restraints."[25]

A transcendent approach may sound like a good idea, allowing for the principles of the Constitution to emerge, but it is not without its inherent weaknesses. A common judicial question when discussing any American right or doctrine is *Where do you find that in the Constitution?* What clause or phrase indicates that the right exists or that your construction of a principle is the correct one? This is no small question, because a Constitution is meant to be a national charter we can all understand, a clear description of government powers and limits. *Where does the Constitution say that?* is an important question and "somewhere near the back" is not a sufficient answer. "Everywhere" is not a satisfying answer either. The central criticism of a transcendent approach is that it opens the door to interpretations that simply aren't supported by the text. Its virtue is that it allows broader purposes to emerge; its vice is that it opens the document to too much interpretation. Transcendence can allow contemporary readers to find what they want to find, to see what they want to see. Simply put, if the document means a great deal beyond its literal words, it can mean anything, so it might eventually mean nothing. On the other hand, if we only read individual clauses for their specific and limited meaning, the greater goals and purposes of our Constitution may be lost.

Identifying Transcendent Principles

Can transcendence illuminate the meaning and purpose of the Constitution without becoming so open-ended that it destroys the function of a written document? That may be the limiting question of a transcendent approach. If the workable answer is *No*, then a transcendent reading is not viable. If the answer is *Yes*, then it could be a legitimate means of understanding and applying the Constitution. A positive answer seems to rely on two conditions: (1) we can identify transcendent principles that most readers would agree are truly there, and (2) we can limit those principles to a workable set that is established prior to addressing any given case or controversy. If we cannot identify the transcendent values with some degree of broad agreement, then it is doubtful that the approach can be persuasive. Perhaps more importantly, if we cannot limit the transcendent values to those we have identified in a principled fashion prior to beginning deliberations on a specific issue, then the approach is open to the charge that we can find any new transcendent principle as the situation requires. In that sense the desired outcome drives the set of principles rather than the principles determining the proper resolution.

So how would we know which values are transcendent? The most obvious method may be to identify the ideas that are invoked repetitively throughout the document. If we read the Constitution like a novel—from beginning to end, with an eye toward discerning a message or theme—what does the document mean? Perhaps it means that we enshrine the sovereignty of the people rather than control by arbitrary government. Or it means that the goal of government is to protect individual liberty. Or that our goal is to balance these two concerns—popular control with individual rights—what we described earlier as the principle of ordered liberty. Perhaps the leading candidate for a transcendent value is freedom. The Preamble specifically identifies the preservation of liberty as a central goal. The Bill of Rights invokes freedom in several different aspects in multiple amendments. The Ninth Amendment contains perhaps the broadest invocation of liberty, suggesting broad and unspecified freedoms that are reserved to the people. If liberty is the single most significant concept of the Constitution, then it may allow for more and stronger freedoms than the initial ones described in the first eight amendments. If we see liberty as transcendent, then at the very least the benefit of the doubt should go to individual liberty when it is weighed against other considerations. And perhaps it is even more expansive, opening the possibility for liberties beyond the scope of those imagined by the Founders.

However, defining a transcendent principle of freedom may be more difficult than it appears. We have to discern which concept of liberty is enshrined. Earlier we discussed the distinctions between *pure liberty* and *ordered liberty* as a defining principle of the Constitution. If pure liberty is the transcendent value, this creates a much broader realm of individual rights free of restraint by the majority. However, if what the Constitution really suggests is ordered liberty, then there is an appropriate balance between individual rights and the community's concerns for decency or stability. If we read the *Bill of Rights* comprehensively, it may seem as though pure liberty is the transcendent value. If we read the *entire document* comprehensively, balancing the message of the Bill of Rights with the role of democratic government, it may lean toward ordered liberty.

A second candidate for a transcendent principle is *equality*. Like liberty, equality is one of the foundations of our democracy. A system of free elections to determine our leaders inherently suggests equality: one person, one vote. The Constitution also establishes an absolute prohibition against titles of nobility. The old norm under the monarchy—that some people were by definition better than others and had special privileges under the law—is absolutely prohibited in the United States. The Fifth Amendment guarantees due process of law to all persons, which means that everyone faces the same legal system with the same procedures. The Fourteenth Amendment explicitly invokes the equal protection of the laws, meaning that all persons must be treated in the same fashion regardless of distinctions such as race or religion. Legal equality seems to resonate throughout the document, though perhaps not to the same degree as liberty. When the two are compared, most readers conclude that the highest priority is freedom, followed by equality, though this is not universally agreed. The question is important, because even two principles that are both transcendent may still clash with each other, creating a tension that is irresolvable unless we know ahead of time which one has the greater value.

In addition to liberty and equality, a case could be made for other transcendent values such as justice. The Preamble specifically mentions establishing justice as a goal, and the Bill of Rights focuses a great deal of attention on the rights of citizens facing criminal prosecution by the state, including the broad right of due process. However, this principle is harder to justify than either liberty or equality, which brings us back to the threshold problem of knowing when a principle qualifies. If the threshold is too low and the list of transcendent principles has no established ending, then the concept can be watered down to the point that it has no meaning.

Another line of thinking about transcendence does not begin with liberty, but with a different principle: the preservation of the constitutional order. Perhaps the highest value of the Constitution is preserving the system established by the Constitution, or in other words, maintaining a government that promotes liberal democracy in a world that often degenerates into disorder and tyranny. In this view, the constitutional order itself is the bulwark against this fate, so its preservation is the greatest good. We must have a surviving democracy or all of our values and freedoms fail, with little chance of future redemption or improvement. The most famous advocate of this idea was Abraham Lincoln. He argued forcefully that he had to break the Constitution in order to preserve it, justifying his actions under color of war that would never be legitimate otherwise. These included imprisoning citizens without trial and suspending *habeus corpus*, the constitutionally protected right to claim a judicial proceeding to ensure that due process is followed.

Other prominent advocates of this transcendent principle of the Constitution include Judge Richard Posner (one of the most well-known contemporary conservative legal minds) and Thomas Jefferson. Though Jefferson advocated limited federal power, while in office he followed a different path. His justification for negotiating the Louisiana Purchase outside of the authority of the Constitution was that "a strict observance of the written laws is doubtless *one* of the high duties of a good citizen, but it is not *the highest*. The laws of necessity, of self-preservation, of saving our country when in danger, are of higher obligation. To lose our country by a scrupulous adherence to written law, would be to lose the law itself, with life, liberty, property and all those who are enjoying them with us; thus absurdly sacrificing the end to the means."[26] The Supreme Court has agreed with this sentiment on more than one occasion in dealing with war powers and national threats. In support of the ability of the federal government to enforce mandatory military service regardless of potential violations of individual rights, the Court asserted that "while the Constitution protects against invasions of individual rights, it is not a suicide pact."[27] In *Dennis v. U.S.*, the free speech case that introduced the "clear and present danger" test for legitimate restrictions of speech under the First Amendment, the Court ruled that "if a society cannot protect its very structure from armed internal attack, it must follow that no subordinate value can be protected."[28] This is a distinct version of transcendence: simply put, we must first protect the system before we can perfect it.

These perspectives create a set of possibilities for identifying and prioritizing transcendent values:

A. Liberty (either Pure or Ordered), stop
B. Liberty first, Equality second, stop (liberty trumps equality when in conflict)
C. Equality first, Liberty second, stop (equality trumps liberty when in conflict)
D. Liberty & Equality, something else third, stop
E. Options A, B, C, or D + Preservation
F. Preservation first + Options A, B, C, or D

These possibilities represent different views of how transcendence should be focused or limited. The longer the list of transcendent principles, the broader the influence they have. However, the shorter the list, the more legitimate and powerful the approach is because it cannot be expanded arbitrarily at the whim of a current majority of Justices. Whether we focus on liberty or preservation as the highest value takes us in two different directions. Preservationist transcendence, which empowers the president to take extraordinary actions to defend the Republic, is in direct contradiction to libertarian transcendence, which suggests broad individual freedoms that cannot be violated even under extreme conditions. Transcendence can be a powerful means of reading the Constitution, but it can lead to several different outcomes.

The Past and Future of Transcendence

This point of conflict shapes constitutional thinking while remaining relatively quiet compared to the other disputes. It is highly influential but most often not acknowledged. Like the other points of conflict, it has a history in the Court's precedents, especially in the rulings on privacy rights. The concept of privacy as a constitutional liberty is a broad freedom perhaps best defined by Justice Louis Brandeis as "the right to be let alone—the most comprehensive of rights and the right most valued by civilized men."[29] This is a well-worn quote from his dissent in *Olmstead v. New York* in 1928, the case that upheld the constitutionality of wiretapping, a relatively new innovation of that time. From these origins, privacy was applied to the regulation of contraception and then to abortion restrictions. In *Griswold v. Connecticut* in 1965 the Court argued that rights have shadows or emanations that expand their scope, which they famously called "penumbras" ("the First Amendment has a penumbra where privacy is protected from governmental intrusion ... specific guarantees in the Bill of Rights have penumbras, formed by emanations from those guarantees that help give them life and substance").[30] The term *penumbra* is often used to describe an eclipse and the outer parts of its shadow; hence it implies the radiance of a powerful object, like the Sun or the Constitution.

The term was also ridiculed in subsequent years and this line of reasoning was dropped in favor of the fundamental rights approach discussed in chapter 3. The Court found privacy to be a fundamental right, located in the Due Process Clause of the Fourteenth Amendment. At the time of the Founding and throughout the 1800s, due process was understood as a *procedural* protection. This meant that the legal process in any criminal proceeding or administrative action taken by the government had to be normal, following the usual procedures that apply to everyone. Whenever an individual faced the large and powerful government, it had to play fair, with no arbitrary actions or decisions that were not conducted openly and applied to everyone. The contemporary expansion of this clause beyond the clear procedural concerns of traditional due process can be understood as a means of enacting a transcendent approach while seeming to identify a specific location within the document.

One of the clearest expressions of transcendent liberty came in the 2003 *Lawrence* ruling, which expanded gay rights by striking down the Texas sodomy law. In this landmark decision the Court invoked the "liberty of the person both in its spatial and more transcendent dimensions," one of the rare uses of the word itself. Justice Kennedy ends his ruling with some of the best writing found in the Court's recent decisions:

Had those who drew and ratified the Due Process Clauses of the Fifth Amendment or the Fourteenth Amendment known the components of liberty in its manifold possibilities, they might have been more specific. They did not presume to have this insight. They knew times can blind us to certain truths and later generations can see that laws once thought necessary and proper in fact serve only to oppress. As the Constitution endures, persons in every generation can invoke its principles in their own search for greater freedom.[31]

Lawrence v. Texas is controversial and its future is unclear. Whether or not the Court will embrace the concept of transcendent liberty is one of the great questions facing the current bench. It is worth noting that one Justice wrote a two-paragraph dissent to *Lawrence* specifically to say that transcendent rights do not exist. If the concept can be developed in a limited and specific way that creates a practical means of applying broad rights to specific conflicts, then it may continue as an important constitutional doctrine. If not, it may go the way of penumbras after a fleeting existence. The distinction between *libertarian* and *preservationist* transcendence is also likely to be addressed further, as future cases invoke war powers in responses to terrorism or other broad threats to our society. At this point it is unclear if liberty or preservation will be considered the highest transcendent value, especially when the two come into direct conflict.

Before moving on to the next chapter, it is important to note that we have reached the final point of conflict grounded in constitutional principle. These five conflicts include the nature of rights, the role of federalism, the definition of liberty, the question of a religious foundation of our system, and, finally, the acceptance or rejection of transcendence (and in which form). We can see now that several of these principles work together harmoniously. Collective rights, federalism, and ordered liberty tend to group together. Collective rights are often expressed at the state level, which is supported by federalism. And both of these concepts are often employed to uphold standards of decent behavior valued by the community, the essence of ordered liberty as opposed to pure liberty. But if liberty is pure rather than ordered, this dovetails with individual rights and a resistance to federalism. The Fourteenth Amendment may have altered rights to be individual and simultaneously eliminated federalism as an important constitutional doctrine, enshrining pure liberty as the new standard for our society. The first group of perspectives on collective rights, federalism, and ordered liberty fit well with a religious foundation of the Constitution, especially in regard to pre-existing natural rights, which the document protects but does not create. On the other hand, a secular document allows for a more evolving perception of rights, which fits with the growth of pure liberty. Finally, the first collection of perceptions tends to match with either a rejection of transcendence or a perception that the highest transcendent value is the preservation of the Constitution; the second group grounded in individual rights supports a perception of transcendent liberty. Constitutional beliefs do not have to fit together in these bundles, and there are many ways of making sense of different combinations of perspectives. The important point is that they are not fully independent, but instead influence and interact with each other.

The next point of conflict is not about principle but about premise. Now we move outside of the Constitution itself into the realm of social facts, which the Supreme Court may try to avoid but clearly cannot.

8

SOCIAL FACTS

Should the Supreme Court Move Ahead of Society or Wait for Social Change?

The most obvious role of the Supreme Court may be to resolve questions of constitutional principle, but the Court is also drawn into disputes over how we define certain social realities. The Court's decisions rarely acknowledge this role, nor have the Justices developed a body of doctrine to guide their rulings on social facts. Nonetheless, the interaction of the enduring principles of our Constitution with the changing facts of our society cannot be avoided. Social facts are especially important in the recurring questions surrounding our definition of a legal person. In the Bong Hits case discussed in the first chapter, the dispute over free speech reflected a fundamental disagreement on whether minors are the same as adults or in a distinct category of their own. Perhaps the most important recurring question to come before the Court is *Who is a full person with all legal rights?* The Court's answers in the realm of race, gender, and abortion—that women and African Americans gained status as legal persons and fetuses did not—is one way to characterize some of the most significant and controversial developments in the last century of constitutional interpretation.

"Persons in the Whole Sense": The Evolving Definition of Legal Personhood

An ardent Communist once said at his trial, "Communists do not murder people." This clear falsehood is noteworthy for the ways it could be believed to be true. Perhaps the most obvious interpretation of the statement is that it is a self-serving lie, meant as an ideological dodge for the crimes of the early Leninists and Stalinists as well as the later leaders of the Soviet Union and in this case East Germany.[32] But there are at least two ways that it could be understood to be true. The first is that their acts of killing were not murder, but instead something else such as self-defense or legitimate state executions. A second and potentially more interesting way in which the statement could be true is that the objects killed were not people. If they were non-persons, the statement is again true. In the Soviet era, the Russian government employed the category of official non-person, the term for those who were not recognized by the state as having a legitimate existence, such as dissidents or other undesirables. The Orwellian term for this status in *1984*'s Newspeak is *unperson*, reflecting his criticism of the totalitarian trends of that era.

In the Anglo-American legal tradition, a person is not merely any human, but a human with all of the rights and obligations of membership in the community. Persons can exercise all of their rights and can be called upon to perform all of their duties.[33] A legal person is a category both more expansive and restrictive than all human beings: there are *persons who are not humans* as well as *humans who are not persons*. The classic case of the first category is a corporation, often described as "a person without a soul." To take a random example, a corporation such as Vandelay Industries can own property, make contracts, and be a party to lawsuits as if it were a person, though this is a recognized legal fiction.[34] The classic case of a human who is not a full legal person is a child; minors cannot be held accountable for several legal purposes nor claim political rights to free speech or assembly, though they do not lack several other rights that attach to being human. In the history of American law, the boundaries of personhood have been a question of great contention, reflecting this crucial distinction between people and persons. The important questions are which categorizations we see as legitimate or obvious and how they evolve over time.

Justice Blackmun in *Roe v. Wade* employs the phrase "persons in the whole sense." This formulation illustrates a crucial point in the evolution of personhood—that the category is not an absolute, which would suggest that an individual either is or is not a person in regard to all considerations. Instead, an individual can be a person for some proceedings and still not be in regard to others. Individuals are not necessarily persons absolutely, but are *persons for a given purpose*. Hence children are persons for some but not all purposes, a status that once also applied to minorities and to women.

A popular bumper sticker of the women's movement reads, "Feminism is the Radical Notion That Women are People." This formulation sounds natural and even irrefutable in our cultural time, but this masks a broader historical point that women holding full status as legal persons *is* a radical idea, which is to say that it emerged only within the most recent era of human history and only became normal within the last hundred years. This is reflected in the evolution of constitutional rulings regarding the nature of women. In 1872 three Justices stated:

> the civil law, as well as **nature herself**, has always recognized a wide difference in the respective spheres and destinies of man and woman... The **natural** and proper timidity and delicacy which belongs to the female sex evidently unfits it for many of the occupations of civil life. The constitution of the family organization, which is **founded in the divine ordinance**, as well as in **the nature of things**, indicates the domestic sphere as that which properly belongs to the domain and functions of womanhood.[35]

This view was upheld in the 1908 landmark case of *Muller v. Oregon*, in which all nine Justices ruled:

> That woman's physical structure and the performance of maternal functions place her at a disadvantage in the struggle for subsistence is **obvious**... history discloses **the fact that** woman has always been dependent upon man... there is that in her disposition and habits of life which will operate against a full assertion of those rights... The reason runs deeper, and rests upon **the inherent difference** between the two sexes.[36]

Note the use of language such as "natural," "the fact that," and the "obvious" or "inherent" "nature of things." These terms suggest that the Court ruled upon the Justices' conception of what was obvious at that time. What is obvious at a different time may not be the same. The Court's view in *Muller* was overruled in 1976 in *Craig v. Boren*, which held that the position of women can no longer be decided by "old notions of role typing," nor "archaic and overbroad generalizations," nor "increasingly outdated misconceptions concerning the role of females."[37] In 1996 the Court recognized the full standing of female citizens in *U.S. v. Virginia*, which disallowed the long-standing policy of all-male admissions to Virginia Military Institute, ruling that law or policy must not "deny to women, simply because they are women, full citizenship stature—equal opportunity to aspire, achieve, participate in and contribute to society based on their individual talents and capacities." Government "must not rely on overbroad generalizations about the different talents, capacities, or preferences of males and females."[38]

The Court's rulings on the status of African Americans followed a similar trajectory, from the obvious perception of non-persons at the time of *Dred Scott* to the equally obvious status of full persons at the time of *Brown*. The Court famously ruled in 1857 in *Dred Scott v. Sandford* that slaves and their descendents were "beings of an inferior order, and altogether unfit to associate with the white race, either in social or political relations; and so far inferior, that they had no rights which the white man was bound to respect."[39] For this reason, blacks were ruled to be incapable of citizenship. This perception was overturned in 1954 in *Brown v. Board of Education of Topeka*, which ruled explicitly that blacks "have achieved outstanding success in the arts and sciences as well as in the business and professional world," and that they could no longer be allotted different educational opportunities within the boundaries of the Fourteenth Amendment's guarantee of equal protection of all persons.[40] The ruling implicitly accorded all minorities their full and equal standing as persons.

In the case of both women and minorities, the Court's judgments of personhood were announced as obvious reflections of the Justices' or the public's perceptions. While the underlying attributes that determined partial or full personhood remained unidentified, the concept that stands out in the discussions is *the degree of independence*. The significance of independence as a defining attribute of personhood contributed to policies designed to reinforce the dependency of freed slaves, such as the prohibitions on education. As the educated and independent status of blacks in America became manifest, this basis for denying personhood diminished and then disappeared. The discussion of the personhood of women likewise revolved around the question of independence. The Court's 1908 pronouncement in *Muller* concentrates on this aspect of social relations: "looking at it from the viewpoint of the effort to maintain an independent position in life, she is not upon an equality ... she still looks to her brother and depends upon him. Even though all restrictions on political, personal, and contractual rights were taken away ... it would still be true that she is so constituted that she will rest upon and look to him for protection."[41]

What stands out when examining the constitutional history of personhood is that the same dominant consideration in regard to women and minorities also became the central argument regarding the personhood of a fetus. Unlike for women and minorities, the question of the status of a fetus did not come before the Court several times and slowly evolve toward personhood. The question came before the Court in *Roe v. Wade* in 1973 and was ruled decisively in the negative. The standard that *Roe* applied was viability, defined as the point at which a fetus can survive on its own independent of the mother. In other words, independent standing is the basis of personhood. Because a fetus is not yet independent it does not have the rights of persons, which allowed the ruling in *Roe* to proceed. On the recurring question of personhood, the Court's answers have been that women and African Americans gained status as legal persons while fetuses have not, which is one way to summarize some of the most important rulings of the last century.

How Should the Court Rule on Social Facts?

We can count on new disputes about evolving premises to arrive at the Supreme Court in the future. A social fact that the Court will likely be called on to resolve is the nature of marriage. The U.S. Code currently reads:

> In determining the meaning of any Act of Congress, or of any ruling, regulation, or interpretation of the various administrative bureaus and agencies of the United States, the word "marriage" means only a legal union between one man and one woman as husband and wife, and the word "spouse" refers only to a person of the opposite sex who is a husband or a wife. (1 USC §7)

But this definition may not remain for much longer. Given the actions by conflicting state legislatures, state referenda, and emerging legal challenges from individuals, the Court will in all likelihood have to address the dispute. Not only is the nature of marriage at issue, but also the nature of sexuality. Claims to equal protection of the law rely on distinctions grounded in recognized stable categories such as gender or race. Conduct is not protected, while a category distinction that is beyond the control of the individual is. Hence an unavoidable question is whether homosexuality fits this description. The contemporary argument over whether sexuality is an immutable category engenders passionate disagreement and the Court may be in the unenviable position of being asked to define this disputed social fact.

The central question that divides the Justices is whether they should recognize only well-established changes within society or participate in moving society forward. Should the Court's role be limited to endorsing changes that have clearly occurred (as reflected in the decisions of elected legislatures or manifest changes in public opinion), or should the Court be open to expanding the premises of contemporary society? The first view limits the Court to an outsider's role of merely recognizing undisputed facts, while the second sees the Court as a forward-looking institution that can be in the forefront as well as the mainstream of social change.

Some Justices have greater confidence in their ability to discern evolving social premises accurately, while others have little faith in that judgment, believing instead that it should be left to the political branches that represent the people directly. The Justices rarely comment on the basis of social fact rulings, but Sandra Day O'Connor and Antonin Scalia had a long-running dispute over this question. In *Planned Parenthood v. Casey* in 1992, an important decision on abortion law, O'Connor argued that the Court could discern when "facts, or an understanding of facts" has changed; "the Court's Justices are sometimes able to perceive significant facts ... that eluded their predecessors and that justify departures from existing decisions."[42] Scalia, on the other hand, has little such confidence that the Justices can do this without relying on their own political inclinations, which are not reflections of the Constitution but instead of their own ideologies. In Scalia's view, "it is impossible for judges to make 'factual findings' without inserting their own policy judgments, when the factual findings *are* policy judgments."[43]

The heart of the dispute over social facts is which set of premises the Constitution embodies. Is it the well-established conditions of our society or the changes that are under way? The underlying consideration that divides the current Justices can be reduced to the speed of evolution: one group argues that the Court should only recognize but not participate in the emergence of new social facts, while the other group is prone to accept a role for the Court in advancing social facts that are not fully established. If society is going there anyway, why not go there now? On the other hand, if we are sure that we are going there anyway, what is the rush? We could just let the representative branches do the job in the natural course of their legislation. The Justices who believe they should wait for society rather than move ahead of it are implicitly relying on a democratic or majoritarian standard. This approach argues that the role of the Court is to defer whenever possible to our representative institutions and the will of the majority; if there is a premise judgment to be made, our legislatures are the institutions best-equipped to do this in the name of the people who elected them. The opposing view is that the unelected and more thoughtful Justices of the Court are in a better position to determine what the social facts are or should be. At its core, this point of conflict can be reduced to whether the Court should wait for or go ahead of society, a question that is not answered by the text of the Constitution but influences many constitutional disputes.

9

PRECEDENT

When Should We Follow or Break
from the History of the Court?

The Supreme Court is recognized as our interpreter of something sacred but hard to understand. Its past pronouncements on the meaning of the Constitution shape current views, just as its current rulings will shape future views. But the Court has been wrong. Its decisions have been overruled by later Justices and several historical decisions are looked upon as mistakes. Presumably the Court will be wrong again. So, how do we know whether or not to follow the history of the Court?

The attitude toward precedent is a clear division among the Justices. Some believe that precedents should be followed even if the Court would rule differently if the question came before it today; others believe that following past mistakes is an affront to the system and should be corrected whenever possible, even decades later if necessary. The question posed in the introduction was *What do you call a mistake made fifty years ago?* Some say *a precedent*, which should be followed; others say *a mistake*, which should be corrected. The legal term for following precedent is *stare decisis* (STAR-ay deeSIGHsis), which means *that which has been decided*. But the Supreme Court's adherence to its past decisions is entirely self-enforced. Unlike other courts that must follow the rulings of higher courts, for the Supreme Court *there is no higher court to follow*, leaving it free to act as it sees fit.

This brings us to the important concept of *extinguishing* a case versus *distinguishing* a case. If the Court rules that a prior decision was simply wrong and therefore dead, with no further legal force, it has been *extinguished*. If the current case has a different pattern of facts, so that the previous ruling does not apply even though it is still appropriate in its own realm, then that case has been *distinguished*. It does not control the instant case, but is still alive. For example, in the Bong Hits case, the Court did not apply the precedent of *Tinker* (which ruled that disruption is the core standard under the First Amendment for restricting school speech). If they had, then they would likely have said that the banner was not disruptive and therefore its display could not be restricted. The Court did not follow this reasoning, but neither did it overrule *Tinker* and end its influence. They simply said that the facts were different because *Morse* dealt with a drug reference, which created a different concern that allowed for this restriction while keeping the *Tinker* standard in place for other questions. It is important to be clear whether a previous case is being merely distinguished or truly extinguished.

The standards for extinguishing a prior decision are not clear or agreed upon, but there are some general trends that have emerged. They can be summarized in three conditions: 1) *the social facts underlying a ruling have changed*; 2) *the principle was misapplied* (the previous ruling made a mistake in how it was handled); or 3) *the principle has evolved or a new principle has emerged* (the previous case was wrong about the correct principle). The first standard relates to the discussion of social facts in the last chapter. If a majority of Justices now believe that social facts have changed in a way that requires a new ruling, then the old case must be extinguished. They may have arrived at this view by moving ahead of the current premises of our society or by endorsing a social fact that has become clear within the mainstream of our society, but in either case at least five Justices have agreed that the time has come. The *Casey* decision in 1992 provides a rare explicit discussion of the question of evolving social facts and their relation to overruling established precedents. The question at issue in *Casey* was not merely the constitutionality of the regulations on abortion put in place by the state of Pennsylvania, but whether the core holding of *Roe v. Wade* in 1973 would be reconsidered. The ruling written by O'Connor states that "no change in *Roe's* factual underpinning has left its central holding obsolete." She argues that one of the only grounds for abandoning precedent is that "facts have so changed, or come to be seen so differently, as to have robbed the old rule of significant application or justification." Legitimate decisions that have overturned previous rulings did so "on the basis of facts, or an understanding of facts, changed from those which furnished the claimed justifications for the earlier constitutional resolutions. The overruling decisions were comprehensible to the Nation, and defensible, as the Court's responses to changed circumstances."[44] Under these conditions, when the Justices perceive a clearly altered social fact, a precedent may need to be overturned.

The second and third standards relate to principles. Either a recognized principle has been applied wrongly in the past or a new principle has emerged. The reasons for seeing an old or new principle in a certain light could depend on any of the points of conflict we have discussed in previous chapters; it could be a shift in individual versus collective rights, or about federalism, or a changing perception of transcendence, or any of several justifications. The ease with which changes in principle can take place is limited by the strength of the old precedents. Simply put, the more decisions on the books that support the current position and the older those decisions are, the stronger the case for maintaining *stare decisis*. A single obscure ruling from a few years ago is quite different from dozens of well-known rulings stretching across decades.

The heart of the division could be described as concentrating *on the history of the Court versus the history of the Constitution*. The Court's collected rulings may be our most important way of understanding our system. The other perspective is that the history of the Constitution itself is the more important source of information. The first concentrates on constitutional precedent and the second on constitutional principle. Those principles could be found in the immutable meaning of the document or in the evolving meaning of how we have come to understand its growth over time, but in either case it is principles all the way down. The debate can be reduced to *stability versus accuracy*. The more we adhere to the existing precedents, with as little incremental change as possible, the more stable and predictable the law remains. The more we emphasize its inherent or evolving principles, regardless of the current precedents, the more accurate and faithful to the meaning of the Constitution we can be. There is no agreement on whether stability or accuracy creates more legitimacy for the Court.

A fascinating case study in the power of precedent took place in 2000 in the case of *Dickerson v. U.S.* The case challenged the application of the famous *Miranda* ruling to federal trials, which had been excluded from those requirements by an act of Congress. The constitutionality of this practice was challenged by Charles Dickerson, who claimed he had not been given the explicit warning that he had the right to remain silent and to be provided a lawyer for his defense before he made an incriminating statement that led to his conviction for bank robbery, a federal offense. Chief Justice William Rehnquist wrote the Court's decision. This is significant because Rehnquist was on record as believing the initial ruling in *Miranda* was wrong. If the question came to the Court as a fresh case during his tenure, he surely would not have agreed to a decision in any sense like *Miranda*, in which the Court created a new and exacting rule found nowhere in the Constitution. Nonetheless, he wrote: "Whether or not we would agree with *Miranda's* reasoning and its resulting rule, were we addressing the issue in the first instance, the principles of *stare decisis* weigh heavily against overruling it now ... *Miranda* has become embedded in routine police practice to the point where the warnings have become part of our national culture."[45] Two dissenters took the position that *Miranda* was simply wrong, regardless of the passage of time; it was not grounded in the Constitution in 1966 when the ruling was made (as Rehnquist agrees), and is no more legitimate now (which Rehnquist disputes). Precedent can be persuasive, but not infinitely. Where an individual fits along that spectrum heavily influences their way of reading the Constitution.

10

COMPLETENESS

What Else Do We Need to Read?

We began with the conflict over judicial review, or who gets to read and interpret the Constitution for the rest of the nation. We can end with another broad question: *What exactly do they need to read?* The last major question that divides the Supreme Court is whether the document stands alone as a complete and understandable text or whether we must appeal to outside sources to comprehend its meaning and apply it to contemporary society.

We can sketch roughly five common positions that invoke a fully complete to very incomplete Constitution. The most clear position is that the Constitution is a perfect document that stands alone as our national charter. We can understand it as it is offered and to do otherwise is likely to pollute its ideas or simply bring in personal preferences that do not reflect its true meaning. But are we sure that it can be understood on its own? If we need to understand other ideas in order to comprehend it fully, this raises difficult questions about *which* outside sources we take seriously and which we reject.

The second view is that the Constitution has to be understood within the entire framework of the Founding era. This does not mean that the Constitution is incomplete in the sense of needing new ideas or additions, but that in order to understand its meaning we need to know what the Founders were thinking and the influences that shaped our national values. The other sources that inform us about the Founding include the political theory that influenced the Framers (notably Hobbes, Locke, Machiavelli, and Montesquieu); the *Federalist Papers* (which summarize the public debates about the ratification of the Constitution); the Declaration of Independence; the records from the Constitutional Convention; and the biographies of the leading Founders, such as Washington, Jefferson, Madison, Hamilton, Adams, and Franklin. In other words, the greater our knowledge of the Founding era, the more we can understand the ideas and purposes of the Constitution.

A third view is also focused on the Founding, but in a different sense than using the historical sources to understand the Constitution. This perspective argues that there were *two* founding documents rather than just one. The Declaration of Independence should be read alongside the Constitution, framing how we read the later document. If the revolutionary document of 1776 and the governing document of 1787 are the front and back bookends of the Founding era, then both are significant. If the first announces purposes while the second clarifies the means to achieve them, then both are necessary. Whether we do or do not see the Declaration in this light changes how we understand the Constitution. To be clear, the previous view—focused on the Founding era as a whole—includes the Declaration as a part of that worldview, but only as one piece among several; the third view focuses on the Declaration in almost a co-equal relationship to the Constitution in a dual-document understanding of our government.

A fourth view is that the Constitution is meant to embody the evolving beliefs of the American people, so those beliefs must accompany any reading of the document. Grand ideas like liberty and equality take on the meaning of their time, rather than a static or permanent definition. If this is the case, then we must pay attention to the evolution of the public values that may shape our reading of the Constitution. The most contentious part of this position may be its extension to not merely American values but global ones. If the Constitution is meant to reflect universal values, then we may have to pay attention to changes outside the United States.

The final mainstream position is that the Constitution is incomplete in its application to the vast number of unforeseen changes in American society. Therefore the history of the precedents becomes an indispensable tool in reading and interpreting the Constitution. The history of the Supreme Court cases is as important—or perhaps more important—than the text of the document. The division over the power of precedent was discussed in the last chapter, but it can also be seen as an important subset of the question of completeness. When we considered the tradeoff between stability versus accuracy in the interpretation of the document, another way of thinking about this is how much accuracy is provided by the history of the precedents. If the Constitution is complete and understandable by itself, then the precedents do not add and may detract from an accurate reading. However, if the document needs additional clarification, then the accumulated wisdom of many years of the Court's rulings may be a clear way of filling in the gaps.

These five positions on the completeness of the Constitution—from complete, to encompassing the Founding era, encompassing the Declaration, requiring contemporary beliefs, or requiring the history of the precedents—support different schools of thought on the Constitution. Before we move to that discussion in Part II of this volume, a few questions remain about sources outside of the text of the Constitution, especially the role of the Declaration and the nature of evolving American beliefs.

The Role of the Declaration

Many commentators have observed that the Declaration and the Constitution are quite different. The distinction in tenor could be because the first is a revolutionary document while the second is a document for long-term governance. Perhaps the Declaration is addressed to lofty goals while the Constitution is designed for realistic demands; therefore the early document is optimistic while the later one is pessimistic. In order to illustrate some of the distinctions, I would like to play what I call the *Constitution or Declaration Game*. The rules are simple: for each of the well-known phrases below, keep track of which you think appear in the Constitution and which in the Declaration.

"We hold these truths to be self-evident"
"the Laws of Nature and of Nature's God"
"all Men are created equal"
"Life, Liberty, and the Pursuit of Happiness"
"all men are endowed by their Creator with certain unalienable rights"
"oppose with manly firmness invasions of the rights of the People"

The last phrase really shouldn't be there because it is neither famous nor important, but nonetheless I find it amusing. However, it *is* from the Declaration, just like all the rest. None of these statements is found in the Constitution, though every time I discuss them, a good proportion of people think that several of them are. The ideas embedded in these phrases—natural rights endowed by God, the essential equality of man, the individual pursuit of happiness—are explicitly stated in the Declaration, but at best implied in the Constitution. So, why do many of us believe that the Constitution contains words found in the Declaration instead, especially the famous phrase that all men are created equal?

Many historians trace it to the mid-1800s and the Gettysburg Address. Lincoln's speech in 1863 is one of the most famous in American history, perhaps the most influential 268 words ever spoken (compared to the Declaration at over 1,000 and the Constitution at around 5,000). The argument of the speech is not readily available in the minds of most Americans, but the resonance is very much there. Lincoln began with a deceptively profound statement, that "our fathers brought forth on this continent a new nation, conceived in liberty, and dedicated to the proposition that all men are created equal." What was the purpose of the American Founding? It was dedicated to *what*? Constitutional government? Freedom from tyranny? Individual liberty? Lincoln said it was something else—the essential equality of humans—which derives from the Declaration, not the Constitution. He connected this purpose to the constitutional order—"government of the people, by the people, for the people"—in a way that has remained in our national consciousness.

In his other writings, Lincoln employed the metaphor from Proverbs 25 of the golden apple in the silver frame:

> Without the Constitution and the Union, we could not have attained the result; but even these are not the primary cause of our great prosperity. There is something else back of these, entwining itself more closely about the human heart. That something is the principle of "Liberty to all." ... The assertion of that principle ... has proved an "apple of gold" to us. The Union, and the Constitution, are the picture of silver, subsequently framed around it. The picture was made, not

to conceal, or destroy the apple; but to adorn, and preserve it. The picture was made for the apple—not the apple for the picture.[46]

In the following decades of the late 1800s and throughout the 1900s, the Declaration emerged as a core document of our culture, a position it had not held previously. The rhetorical substitution of the Declaration for the Constitution as the primary definition of our system can be traced to the Civil War and Gettysburg. Contemporary readers of the Constitution have been influenced by this rise of the Declaration's status, but some more than others.[47]

So what are the implications of reading the Constitution in light of the Declaration? The meaning of the Gettysburg Address is that the goal of our system is to achieve equality—the argument of the Declaration—rather than to preserve liberty, which is the central argument of the Constitution. Both are core values of our democracy, but the balance of the two, especially when they come into conflict, is one of our enduring internal battles. The primacy of one value over the other has everything to do with whether we read the Constitution with the guiding purpose of the Declaration in mind or not.

But that is not all: if we bring in the Declaration, then we bring in the whole thing. The dripping religiosity of the Declaration stands in contrast to the secular language of the Constitution. This reinforces a religious reading of the document in addition to the focus on equality. The equality invoked in the Declaration is firmly grounded in the natural rights tradition—not the evolved equality of changing social conditions, but the eternal equality granted by God. Natural Law is a major facet of the Declaration that reinforces this interpretation of rights under the Constitution.

The Role of Evolving American Beliefs

A different view of an incomplete Constitution focuses on the evolving beliefs of Americans. The broad values invoked in the Constitution—democratic representation, liberty, equality, justice—meant one thing at the time of the Founding, but those same words and ideas have different meanings now. For example, at the time the Constitution was ratified, political representation was thought of in a limited way, exerted by a small group of the property holders. From a much more elitist origin we have adopted a newer ideal of representation grounded in broad citizen participation. The same applies to the concept of liberty. The ordered liberty of the Founding may have been eclipsed by the newer vision of pure liberty discussed in chapter 5.

One way of phrasing the question of completeness is whether important cultural documents of our more recent history should be taken into account in reading the Constitution. One of the most influential contemporary definitions of liberty comes from John Stuart Mill. Though written by an Englishman, *On Liberty* has become one of the most frequently cited definitions of freedom in our culture. The idea that individual liberty includes the ability to act as one chooses until reaching the border of direct harm to another citizen has become perhaps the most widely accepted view. The question that divides readers of the Constitution is whether the argument of *On Liberty* counts as a *cultural view* or a *constitutional view*. If it is the first, then it could be influential on the actions of voters, legislators, governors, or presidents; if it is the second, then the Justices should incorporate it into their interpretation of constitutional liberty.

Beyond the evolution of American beliefs there is an even more contentious question about the opinions of the broader world. Some Justices have begun to look upon foreign precedents as meaningful, a practice that is violently opposed in some quarters. If the United States is interwoven with a larger set of Western democracies, then perhaps we should take their views seriously. On the other hand, if we are unique as the leading rather than following voice of constitutional democracy, then perhaps we should not consider outside sources of law and values. The most well-known decision that invokes foreign precedent is the 2003 *Lawrence* ruling that invalidated sodomy laws, overruling the 1986 *Bowers* decision: "To the extent *Bowers* relied on values we share with a wider civilization, it should be noted that the reasoning and holding in *Bowers* have been rejected elsewhere. The European Court of Human Rights has followed not *Bowers* but its own decision in *Dudgeon v. United Kingdom* ... Other nations, too, have taken action consistent with an affirmation of the protected right of homosexual adults to engage in intimate, consensual conduct."[48] One of the opponents of citing foreign precedent, Chief Justice John Roberts, referred to the practice during his confirmation hearings as "looking out over a crowd and picking out your friends." Few Americans who support the use of European precedents for gay rights would agree that the decisions of European courts were a valid source for rulings on protections from intrusive government searches or police wiretaps, given that few such protections exist under European law. But a principled position on foreign precedent would see all or none of it as worthy of consideration.

A Final Word on Points of Conflict

With the question of completeness we come to the end of our discussion of the nine points of conflict that shape how we read the Constitution. The next project is to apply these ideas to understanding the four major schools of thought in constitutional interpretation. Whether the approach of Textualism, Common Law Constitutionalism, Originalism, or Living Constitutionalism makes intuitive sense to each reader depends largely on how one reacts to the points of conflict we have discussed. Each point of conflict is an underlying element of the distinct ways of reading the Constitution. Some of the conflicts are more important for one school of thought than another, but each plays an important role. For example, the competing views of completeness are each associated with one particular approach. If the Constitution is complete in and of itself, this leads toward Textualism. If it requires an understanding of the Founding era as a whole, this supports an Originalist reading. A focus on the evolving beliefs of contemporary Americans leads toward Living Constitutionalism. And relying on the history of the precedents as an integral part of the Constitution is the foundation of a Common Law approach. Each of these four schools of thought will become clear in the next section of the book, but before delving into each one it will be helpful to consider where you fall on each of the nine points of constitutional conflict (summarized in Table 2.1 on page 24). Your initial inclinations or gut reactions to these will shape to a remarkable extent which of the four schools of thought appeals to you. With these conflicts in mind, the schools of thought, the famous cases, and the future disputes will all become clear.

Part II

SCHOOLS OF
INTERPRETATION

11

TEXTUALISM

The Constitution may be our clearest definition of what we are as a people, yet how we read it leads to very different conclusions. Four major schools of thought, or ways of reading the document, define the boundaries of our constitutional controversies. Each school of interpretation has virtues and flaws. None is without criticism. From the perspective of a citizen attempting to understand the Constitution in the most legitimate and accurate way, perhaps the best means of comprehending each approach is through the positions each takes on the nine points of conflict we have discussed.

Constitutional questions do not always reflect the same politics of liberal versus conservative ideologies that characterizes our contemporary political issues, but we nonetheless speak of a left and a right of the Supreme Court. If we arrange the four schools of interpretation in terms of how they are usually seen on a left (liberal) to right (conservative) spectrum, it looks like this:

Living Constitutionalism	Common Law Constitutionalism	Textualism	Originalism

The two approaches at the far ends—Living Constitutionalism and Originalism—are clearly opposed in their views of the Constitution, but the two in the middle share perhaps the second largest antagonism. Textualism and Common Law Constitutionalism take conflicting approaches to reading the Constitution, creating conflict in the middle as well as at the ends of the spectrum. We will discuss each school in turn, focusing on how they believe the Constitution should be read, how their views are shaped by the underlying points of conflict, and the weaknesses that each perspective carries. No legitimate writer could claim that one is absolutely correct without question or flaw. Nonetheless we have to choose, because life is like this—there is no perfect answer, yet an answer must be had.

How to Read the Constitution: Textualism

Textualists argue that the most clear and legitimate means of understanding the Constitution is to focus on the words themselves. A brilliant document written by brilliant men needs no additions, translations, or outside forces to understand it. It was written to be read and understood by our citizens—written by and for the people themselves. No classes of specialists or lawyers are necessary. Some degree of work and reading is required, but not to the extent that we must hand over our judgment to anointed experts, especially when they claim that something that clearly says X actually means Y (if you have the correct sensibilities). We all can and should understand our own document. This is possible because the Constitution simply means what it says and says what it means.

The most well-known advocate of Textualism is Justice Antonin Scalia. Since his appointment to the Supreme Court by President Reagan in 1986, Scalia has been a one-man show expanding the influence of this school of thought. In his approach, each ruling of the Supreme Court must be grounded in the *text, structure, and history* of the Constitution, in that order. The *text* is always the primary consideration. The *structure* of the Constitution is also important because how the parts of the text fit together and relate to each other tells us about the principles of the document. For example, the terms *federalism* or *separation of powers* are not found in the document, but the structure of the national government into distinct but overlapping branches, as well as the division of powers between the national and state governments, indicates that these principles are there. The final consideration, the *history* of the Constitution, means that we should pay attention to the ideas expressed in the Founding era and to the precedents of the Court, but only as a route to understanding the Constitution when the text alone is insufficient. The text and structure trump any understanding of the history or precedent. In no sense should a previous decision or interpretation of the Founding replace the clear meaning of the document's language. The essence of a written Constitution is that it binds us to its meaning. This is not the same as being unchanging, for we have changed it several times (27 to be precise), but we must alter it through amendment as it was intended to be done. Otherwise it continues to mean what it says, regardless of whether we want it to or not. Clever arguments that its meaning has changed will not do. We are bound by the words unless we change them.

Until then they have their common language meaning. In Scalia's phrase, the text contains "all that it fairly means."[49] The words are not meant to be read narrowly or read broadly, but simply fairly, as a common citizen would read them. For example, the First Amendment explicitly protects freedom of speech and of the press. It does not specifically mention messages on signs at a political protest, which are neither explicit speech nor the newspapers or magazines of the press. Nonetheless, a Textualist would argue that political expressions on signs held by individuals at a protest are protected by the First Amendment because a fair reading of its meaning includes political expressions. This example illustrates how Textualism is not the same as the older argument for what was called *strict construction*. This is the view that the Constitution creates only the specific government powers that are described but nothing at all that is not stated explicitly; all questions should be answered as strictly as possible. Textualism opposes this overly narrow reading just as it opposes an overly broad reading that creates concepts or principles that are not there.

An example of this second type of error—inserting meaning into the Constitution that is not present in the text—would be the expansion of the Due Process Clause of the Fourteenth Amendment to include concepts like privacy, which may be valued by citizens but are simply not within the common language meaning of the Constitution. Due process is traditionally understood as a *procedural* protection. This means that any action by the government has to follow the usual procedures that apply to everyone. Whenever we face the large and powerful government, it has to play fair, taking no hidden or arbitrary actions. However, in the early 1900s some legal scholars began to argue that due process was not merely procedural but had a substantive component—the requirements of justice that the procedures were meant to produce. The phrase *substantive due process* has drawn criticism from the beginning; *substantive process* seems to be a contradiction. Due process always meant that everyone must be treated fairly, but no specific outcome was guaranteed. The language of the Due Process Clause provides no guidance as to what a substantive content might be. Possible answers can only be supplied by sources outside of the Constitution, most frequently from the moral or political ideals of the Justices themselves.

The first well-recognized use of the substantive due process doctrine by the Supreme Court was to enforce the property rights of slaveowners. In the infamous case of *Dred Scott* in 1857 the Court insisted that removing a citizen's property was a violation of due process, grounded in its outcome rather than any specific procedure. Property rights to slaves are the opposite of the sort of rights that contemporary Americans believe are protected by a broad doctrine of freedom, which illustrates that the content of substantive due process is open to a wide range of ideas. The next notable instance was the *Lochner* case in 1905.[50] Again, the Court upheld an economic right, in this case invalidating a state law limiting the length of a work week for certain occupations. The Court held that this violated the right of contract found in the substantive component of the Due Process Clause, a view that has been widely discredited. *Dred Scott* and *Lochner* are cited frequently as two of the most recognized errors in the history of the Court. They are also clear examples of reasoning that a Textualist would see as illegitimate. The more recent decisions finding a non-textual right to privacy in the Fourteenth Amendment fall into the same category. Regardless of its ideological origin on the left or right, the effort to add to or subtract from the textual meaning of the Constitution is always wrong.

One of the most important instances of a Textualist approach leading toward the liberal side of the Court was in the flag burning case of *Texas v. Johnson*, mentioned earlier in the introduction. Scalia has no love for flag burners, but sincerely believes that the First Amendment does not allow restrictions of political speech, including offensive kinds. Scalia also sided against the conservatives on questions of detaining enemy combatants in the war on terror. The text of the Constitution authorizes Congress to suspend the writ of habeus corpus, which would then allow for the detention of citizens without trial. But if Congress does not do so openly and in the prescribed way, then the executive branch cannot simply act on its own. A Textualist might personally approve of a government action and yet still believe the text of the Constitution does not allow it.

Points of Conflict

Of the nine points of constitutional conflict, some stand out as defining elements of each school of thought. For Textualism it is *completeness*, *precedent*, and *transcendence*. Textualists take the strong position that the Constitution is complete and perfect on its own. The language is understandable in its ordinary meaning. This stands in sharp contrast to approaches that see a substantial knowledge of the precedents (Common Law) or of the Founding era (Originalism) or of evolving American beliefs (Living Constitutionalism) as necessary to understand the document. Textualism rejects all of these notions, especially the ideas of organic evolution and judicial creativity. The document can be changed by *us* through amendment, but does not change on its own. The words have a stable meaning specifically because they are meant to bind the government against tyrannical action. Evolving American beliefs do not alter the Constitution on their own until we do it officially.

An approach grounded in the text also means that the *precedents* are not of great value. We should never follow an errant prior decision if it goes against the clear meaning of the document. Rules or legal notions created by the Justices to fit their own intentions have no force compared to the commands of the document. The text is always primary and the value of the precedents is only to clarify new circumstances as a secondary reference at best.

Following the text also suggests that the concept of *transcendence* is heavily suspect. The words are meant to be read plainly rather than with ideas about their expansive meaning. A transcendent reading is neither necessary nor supported by the text when we simply read the words for what they clearly offer. Perhaps more importantly, any transcendent reading opens up the possibility of inserting our own beliefs into the document. In the Textualist view, a limited and objective reading has more legitimacy than a broader but fully subjective one. At its heart, *Textualism is grounded in a high regard for completeness and a negative view of precedent and transcendence.*

At first it may seem that a Textualist approach insists that American society must remain rigid or static, but this would be a misleading conclusion. Textualism only insists that our courts are not the appropriate routes to social change; the normal political process should make those changes when the people demand them. Our representatives in Congress and in the state legislatures have that authority, but not unelected judges deciding to make social policy through perceived changes in the Constitution. In this sense Textualism places a high degree of faith in the democratic process rather than the legal process. Legislatures and courts have distinct roles, with the main power residing with the peoples' representatives. The result of what Scalia calls a "Mr. Fix-It mentality" on the Supreme Court has been to take power from the people and place it where it does not belong. Textualists insist that the essential tenor of the Constitution is to establish democratic institutions. If Congress does something stupid, we should make *them* fix it rather than encouraging the Justices to do so. As Scalia phrases it, "Congress can enact foolish statutes as well as wise ones and it is not for the courts to decide which is which."[51] Who has the ultimate power in our system? The people do, not the judges. Who can understand the meaning of the Constitution? Everyone can, not only the Justices of the Supreme Court.

The judge and legal philosopher Learned Hand, perhaps the most well-known American judge who never sat on the Supreme Court, once said:

> this much I think I do know—that a society so riven that the spirit of moderation is gone, no court *can* save; that a society where that spirit flourishes, no court *need* save; that in a society which evades its responsibility by thrusting upon the courts the nurture of that spirit, that spirit in the end will perish.[52]

In other words, *judicial review infantilizes the public* and therefore the democratic process. In many ways, Textualism can be understood as a *power-denying* rather than *power-grasping* judicial philosophy. The main Textualist criticism of both Common Law and Living Constitutionalist perspectives is that they hand over too much power to judges, taking it away from citizens. When we remember that judicial review is not sanctioned by the text of the Constitution but was a power seized by the Supreme Court, it follows that Textualists would want it to be as limited as possible. For similar reasons, Textualism sees decisions on *evolving social facts* as being in the realm of democratic politics and legislatures rather than Justices and courts. Whenever possible, changes in our working premises should be decided democratically. When Justices take that power unto themselves democracy is lessened.

Weaknesses

No approach to reading the Constitution is without flaws. Textualism offers a strong standard for how the document should be understood, but perhaps this is also its weakness when the meaning of the words is imprecise. In many places the Constitution offers broad principles rather than detailed discussions. When these principles are applied to new circumstances, the document may not offer sufficient guidance. Most Textualists agree that when the text is insufficient, a reader should default to a perspective that is as restrained and as grounded in the text as possible, almost always Originalism. The broader meaning of the text as understood by the Founders gives the best guidance on how to apply it to current circumstances, especially when compared to Common Law or Living Constitutionalist approaches that diverge significantly from the text itself.

Perhaps the greatest difficulty for a Textualist approach is the Ninth Amendment. The language of the amendment clearly suggests that there are rights outside of those specifically detailed in the document ("The enumeration in the Constitution, of certain rights, shall not be construed to deny or disparage others retained by the people.") From a Textualist perspective, what could the Ninth Amendment mean? Its exact meaning can't be determined, so it seems to mean nothing. But it can't mean nothing because according to Textualist doctrine, as well as the normal conventions of reading the Constitution, every part of the document is meaningful. So it can't mean anything and yet it can't mean nothing. This is a sincere problem for a Textualist approach. Some Textualists argue that the Ninth is symbolic, which is to say it invokes the idea of outside sources of rights, such as natural rights, but is only doing so as a gesture or teaching moment without carrying a specific meaning. Many readers do not find this to be a satisfying answer. I believe what Textualists are really offering is a tradeoff: by following this approach the Ninth loses meaning while the rest of the document gains a very clear meaning. The alternative is accepting a murky meaning of the entire document including the Ninth.

Textualism does not hold itself up to be a perfect standard, but more than perhaps any other approach it makes a strong claim to being a *clear* standard. It embraces its clarity in return for its flaws. The tradeoff is there, but it may be well worth taking. Scalia argues that even if his standard is imperfect, he has one, while the other approaches (especially Common Law and Living Constitutionalism) do not. In this sense Textualism creates a principled and predictable means of understanding the Constitution, grounded in the text over outside influences, allowing for democratic control of important decisions rather than granting broad discretion to unelected Justices. Principle and clarity are important virtues, which Textualism may offer more than other approaches.

12

COMMON LAW
CONSTITUTIONALISM

While Textualism is associated with Antonin Scalia, the Common Law approach is connected most clearly to Sandra Day O'Connor. She joined the Supreme Court in 1981 and served for a quarter of a century. Most of that time was with Scalia, who joined the bench five years after O'Connor. The two maintained a philosophical rivalry that occasionally broke into open criticism in the written decisions of the Court. The core dispute was whether consistency or principle creates the greatest degree of legitimacy in reading the Constitution. Justice O'Connor famously argued that "Liberty finds no refuge in a jurisprudence of doubt."[53] This is the opening line of *Planned Parenthood v. Casey* (1992), a ruling upholding many of the abortion regulations instituted by the state of Pennsylvania, but more importantly upholding the essential framework of *Roe* from 1973. The phrase means that consistency in our understanding of the Constitution is of the greatest importance. We must follow precedent and make only minor alterations as events demand because only in this way can citizens have a clear set of expectations about the law. Scalia countered in his dissent in *Casey* that "Reason finds no refuge in this jurisprudence of confusion."[54] This phrase means that a principled approach to reading the Constitution may require us to overturn wrong-headed precedents; we should be consistent with reason rather than with past decisions. The dispute between the two Justices illustrates the core of a Common Law approach: respect for precedent and the adaptation to new circumstances through the incremental addition of new rules.

How to Read the Constitution:
Common Law Constitutionalism

The Common Law challenge emerged in the late 1800s and early 1900s. Like many historical movements, it was a combination of ideas and events. Perhaps the emerging concept that had the greatest influence on the Common Law tradition was evolution. The idea that slow change in a positive direction was natural and inevitable found its way far beyond biology to economics, technology, and social organization. In his famous book on *Constitutional Government* published in 1908, Woodrow Wilson wrote that "government is not a machine, but a living thing ... It is accountable to Darwin, not to Newton."[55] The idea of social evolution dovetailed with American pragmatism, the philosophy that answers had to not only be accurate, but also had to work. High-minded ideals that make us feel good mean little if they do not offer practical solutions to real problems. The events that created problems in the early 1900s were mostly industrialization and urbanization. Around 1920 the United States shifted from a majority rural to a majority urban population, with all that this implies about crowding, crime, poverty, and pollution, or in other words, problems to be solved. Industrialized America presented further issues of regulation, safety, transportation, and unionization. The complexity of modern life demanded new solutions within our constitutional order and Common Law judges intended to provide them.

One way to understand how they aimed to do this is to identify the different forms of law in our legal tradition. We have four distinct types of law, which are often kept separate but Common Law scholars attempted to blend in a distinct way. The first form of law is *statutory law*, or the normal laws passed by legislatures (for example, speeding is illegal and citizens must pay certain taxes). This is what most people have in mind when they think of laws. A second influential form is *natural law*, or essential truths that provide the foundation for individual rights to life and liberty. These do not rely on legislatures to enact them, but were established by God and are upheld by tradition, regardless of the whims of elected officials. The third distinct form of law is the constitutional kind, which reflects an organic act of the people, distinct from either statutory laws that can be reversed by the legislature at any time, as well as natural laws that can be changed by no one.

The final legal form is the *common law*, which fills a particular role in our system. In most European law, judges follow very detailed statutes, with a great deal of learning but very little discretion. In England a different tradition developed, with individual judges adding rulings to handle new circumstances, following the previous decisions but building upon them when necessary. Common law is not a collection of statements by the legislature, nor by God, tradition, or the people, but instead by the long history of judges adding slowly to the body of law. In this sense the law evolves, maintaining its basic shape but changing in small increments. No one judge or legislature controls the outcome, but instead it relies on the collective wisdom of many minds. When we broke from the British, we maintained this system of law, grounded in precedent while building upon it to accommodate new circumstances. *Common Law Constitutionalism is treating constitutional law as if it were common law, applying the same principles and procedures.* Therefore the body of decisions by the Supreme Court defining the Constitution is more relevant than the text of the Constitution itself. We know what the Constitution means through what has been written about it.

One foundation of a Common Law approach is following precedent. The second foundation is incremental change when circumstances dictate. The goal of each addition to the body of constitutional law is a *new workable rule*. Justices should add the smallest change that solves the current problem through a practical solution. The standard is *workability* or the clear practicality of the new Common Law rule. Too little or too feeble a change does not help, and the problem will inevitably come back to the Court; too much or too bold a change upsets the previous balance and will have too many reverberations. The key is a clever and practical solution that alters as little as possible of the stable legal order. In this sense Common Law Constitutionalism can be defined as *tradition plus incremental innovation*. Justice Oliver Wendell Holmes, one of the great advocates of this approach, famously wrote that "the life of the law has not been logic: it has been experience."[56] Rather than appealing to doctrine or principle, he believed we should trust the common stock of wisdom, as expressed in the collective will and judgment of the people over time. *The defining features of Common Law Constitutionalism are precedent, stability, incremental change, and restrained innovation.*

Perhaps one of the best-known examples of Common Law reasoning in recent decisions of the Supreme Court is *Planned Parenthood v. Casey* in 1992. In the 1980s several states enacted restrictions on abortion in keeping with the *Roe* framework that allows the regulation but not the banning of abortion after the first trimester. The question was whether these restrictions went beyond the allowable limits and violated the privacy rights recognized in *Roe. Casey* offers a new standard to answer this question, known as an *undue burden.* Under the new doctrine, a state regulation of abortion is an undue burden—and therefore is impermissible—if it undermines the right to the point of blocking its application. A regulation cannot impose a burden that is unlikely to be overcome, effectively curtailing the right. An undue burden is created if the regulation has "the purpose or effect of placing a substantial obstacle in the path."[57] This approach to constitutional interpretation is the essence of a Common Law perspective: creating a new legal standard that solves the problem at hand by the application of a new workable rule.

The Court applied this standard to four distinct regulations that the Pennsylvania Legislature imposed. Before we discuss the Court's decision, it is instructive to ask whether in your judgment each of these regulations does or does not impose an undue burden as the Court defined it. The first regulation was the requirement for a woman to provide informed consent after hearing a script written by the state. It describes the medical risks of abortion, the availability of adoption services, and suggests literature illustrating the development of the unborn child. (The script employs the phrase "unborn child," which is generally used by those opposing abortion, while "fetus" is generally the term employed by those in favor of abortion rights.) The second regulation was a 24-hour waiting period. A woman seeking an abortion would have to visit a clinic and then return the next day before a procedure could take place. The third regulation was the notification of the parents in the case of a minor. A judge could grant a waiver to this requirement if the minor presented evidence that notification would lead to abuse or violence. The final requirement was that married women notify their spouse, but again a waiver could be granted by a judge. Do each of these regulations create an undue burden or not?

The Court's answer was *No, No, No,* and *Yes.* The first three do not, while the fourth does create an impermissible burden because of the possibility for spousal abuse and retaliation. In O'Connor's view, requiring a woman to officially notify her husband may create a circumstance that blocks the availability of the right. This is distinct from the case of a minor notifying parents because of the lesser degree of rights held by young people and the greater legitimate role of parents as guardians. However, a reasonable person could come to the opposite conclusion, given the more coercive influence of parents over their children. Or one could see all of these regulations as attempts to discourage citizens, especially poor ones, in the case of the delay requirement. Or one could see none of the four requirements as truly blocking the underlying right. The important question from the perspective of a Common Law approach is whether the new rule meets the standard of workability. Does the new rule create predictable, sensible outcomes while altering the surrounding legal framework as little as possible? In one sense the undue burden standard clarified the approach to new abortion regulations, but in another sense it is not clear to our political representatives in state legislatures what would be allowed and what would not. In his dissent in *Casey* Scalia argued that "the ultimately standardless nature of the 'undue burden' inquiry is a reflection of the underlying fact that the concept has no principled or coherent legal basis."[58] In his view the outcome of the new rule is really a reflection of the individual Justices' beliefs and biases rather than a predictable principle; the new Common Law rule is wrong under the Textualist standard of grounding in the Constitution, but is also wrong under the Common Law standard of workability. It is not a coincidence that the strongest objections to the *Casey* ruling came from Scalia, as the Textualist approach (focused on the words alone) and the Common Law approach (focused on precedent and new workable rules created by Justices) are often in direct conflict.

Points of Conflict

Common Law Constitutionalism is grounded in strong positive positions on three of the points of conflict: *precedent, judicial review,* and *social facts.* The heart of the approach is *precedent.* Understanding the Constitution is a matter of comprehending the history of its interpretation. The evolved doctrines of the Supreme Court are the best guide to understand its meaning and to bind our society to a single view.

Perhaps the core virtue of having a constitutional order is that it gives us clear and consistent guidance on what is acceptable and unacceptable. If we change those standards back and forth, it creates a feeling of illegitimacy. If the meaning of the Constitution is uncertain even to the Justices who devote their livers to studying it, then how can it be clear to ordinary citizens? The Justices must place the legitimacy of the Court in front of their own ideological or personal views. Moreover, several generations of Justices working in concert are likely to reach more wise conclusions than any current majority of the Court.

Placing stock in the collective wisdom of the Justices means that *judicial review* must be highly valued. The Constitution does not speak on its own, without the wise intervening judgment of the Supreme Court. The institution of judicial review is not only necessary, but creates far better outcomes than could be achieved by any other approach that has less regard for elite judgment bound by history.

One of the core concerns of judicial review is recognizing evolving *social facts.* The Court should not shy away from its role in determining when new facts have emerged, especially if they alter our understanding of constitutional rights. Awareness of the changing circumstances of society is crucial to the Justices' ability to craft new Common Law rules that solve emerging problems.

A negative view of completeness also reinforces a Common Law approach. If the Constitution is not clear in its principles or in its application to new circumstances without further knowledge, the precedents of the Court fill in these gaps and give the Justices room to craft appropriate responses to emerging conditions. In this view the document is not incomplete in the sense of requiring outside ideas, but in the sense of needing a body of prior interpretations to clarify its nuances. A positive view of precedent and judicial review, a recognition of the need for judicial judgments on evolving social facts, and a doubt about the completeness of the Constitution without the history of judicial decisions to guide us, all lead toward a Common Law approach to reading the Constitution.

Weaknesses

Like Textualism, the central argument of Common Law Constitutionalism may also be its central flaw. Some of the crucial rulings of the

Supreme Court have been simply wrong, and a tremendous regard for precedent can lead to the continuation of negative traditions. One of the difficulties in Common Law reasoning is that it is not clear when precedents should be overturned. Initial decisions on new concerns therefore carry tremendous weight. For example, the original failure to apply the meaning of the Fourteenth Amendment as most scholars believe it should have been applied has led to decades of judicial conflict as the Supreme Court has attempted to maintain the precedents while gaining some of its meaning.

While following precedent is the first element of a Common Law approach, the second foundation is adding new workable rules when the precedents are not sufficient. New Common Law standards may provide plausible responses to current dilemmas, but may not turn out to be as workable as advertised, nor as principled as one might desire. If the new rules cannot be applied effectively by citizens and courts, then they may not fulfill their intended function. It all depends on the wisdom and ability of the Justices, which places a high degree of faith in their judgment. The heart of the disagreement between Scalia and O'Connor reduces to how much they trust our courts versus our citizens. Common Law Constitutionalism places its faith in the history and practice of the Supreme Court as the core means of understanding the Constitution.

13

ORIGINALISM

The Founders would be amazed by many things in contemporary society, but perhaps none more than the continued existence of the Constitution. When he emerged from the Constitutional Convention and was asked by the waiting crowd what kind of government they had, Ben Franklin famously responded, "A Republic, if you can keep it." The fragility of our system—or of any system grounded in a faith in the common people to govern wisely—was foremost in the minds of the Founders. They feared that any free society had to contend with two possible ends: tyranny and anarchy. On the one hand, the people had to withstand the constant pressure toward state oppression, leading to the rebirth of the monarchy or another form of dictatorship; on the other hand, the people had to resist the continual lure of individual freedom without boundaries or responsibilities, leading to social decline and collapse. Franklin was serious when he suggested that it was unlikely that the system would survive. For that reason the Constitution is designed foremost for the preservation of the constitutional order. It is meant to avoid state tyranny more than to create positive liberty, more to avoid the excesses of mob rule and unrestrained individual freedom than to establish a libertarian world of personal choice.

Beginning with the purposes of the Constitution is the essence of an Originalist approach to reading the document. It takes the view that the Constitution is not merely an empty vessel into which we pour our current desires. It has a discernible meaning grounded in specific principles that are at the heart of our national project. *It* has things to teach *us* rather than the reverse. Our evolving beliefs can inform the normal process of political representation, influencing acts of Congress or state legislatures, but our changing values do not alter the meaning of the Constitution and its limits. The Constitution does not protect everything we like and overrule everything we do not. The purpose of a written Constitution—to constrain the government and the people to certain guiding principles and limits—is broken if we believe that our contemporary ideas replace those of the document. The text can be amended, but this is the only legitimate way of altering it. Automatic change through the judgment of the Justices, especially when it overrides the explicit safeguards and limits created by the Constitution, is not acceptable. This is the heart of the argument between Originalists and Living Constitutionalists: do we uphold the values of the document or replace them with our current values; do we cleave to its eternal meaning or our evolving beliefs?

How to Read the Constitution: Originalism

The Founding generation was not immune to disputes over how to read the Constitution in the years following ratification. The issue came up immediately in the public debates over the constitutionality of a Bank of the United States, one of the major controversies in the early days of the Republic. James Madison argued that the intent and meaning in the minds of those who debated and wrote the document should be our guide. Elbridge Gerry, a signer of the Declaration and member of the Constitutional Convention (though he refused to sign the final document because it did not contain a Bill of Rights), argued that "the memories of different gentlemen would probably vary, as they have already done"; therefore the best standard is the language of the document itself.[59] This disagreement would be described today as Originalism versus Textualism. The introduction of Common Law and Living Constitutionalist thinking would not appear for many decades.

John Marshall, the great Chief Justice who wrote *Marbury v. Madison*, did not take a clear position on which of these two views he supported, but his writings reflect some combination of Originalism and Textualism. His famous line in *McCulloch v. Maryland* (1819) is often cited as an endorsement of Living Constitutionalism: "we must never forget that it is a constitution we are expounding," which was "intended to endure for ages to come, and consequently, to be adapted to the various crises of human affairs."[60] This is often taken to mean that we have a Living Constitution, mostly because of the word "adapted." But Marshall's leaning toward Living Constitutionalism has been exaggerated, projecting that perspective back to a time before its creation. Instead he meant that premises change even while principles remain constant, the essential position of Originalism. There is no suggestion in what Marshall wrote that government powers or limits change, only the circumstances to which they apply. In *Gibbons v. Ogden* in 1824 he wrote that "the enlightened patriots, who framed our Constitution, and the people who adopted it, must be understood to have employed words in their natural sense... We know of no rule for construing the extent of powers, other than is given by the language of the instrument which confers them, taken in connexion with the purposes for which they were conferred."[61] This is a combination of Textualism (the language of the instrument) and Originalism (the purposes they intended), which seems to have been Marshall's view. He believed that the principles of the Constitution were immutable; circumstances change and require adaptation of the means of government action but never the ends of our government's purpose.

In 1905 the Court stated the Originalist position clearly in the case of *South Carolina v. U.S.*: "The Constitution is a written instrument. As such its meaning does not alter. That which it meant when adopted, it means now. Being a grant of powers to a government, its language is general; and, as changes come in social and political life, it embraces in its grasp all new conditions which are within the scope of the powers in terms conferred. In other words, while the powers granted do not change, they apply from generation to generation to all things to which they are in their nature applicable. This in no manner abridges the fact of its changeless nature and meaning."[62] In other words, *premises change but principles do not*. This illustrates a common misconception that Originalists in all time periods would make the same ruling because they are looking to the static world of the Founders. Originalists recognize that conditions change. The Founder's principles applied to the social facts of the 1800s create different conclusions than when applied to the circumstances of the present. The idea of Originalism is not to imagine the previous world of powdered wigs and what their wearers would have done; the idea is to understand their principles clearly and apply them to our current society. Static interpretation is a straw man, but while premises change, principles do indeed remain the same. They are not open to change or dismissal merely because we wish it. The entire purpose of a written Constitution is to provide restraints; if those restraints can be ignored or altered at will, the purpose is lost.

Originalism insists that the Constitution has a meaning, grounded in the principles of the Founders, and that this meaning is discernible, grounded in the study of their legacy. To read the Constitution is to study the Founding era and its ideas, which shape the document's passages and provisions even when they are not readily apparent to the casual reader. The meaning of the Constitution is eternal, defining the goals and purposes of our system of government. While social premises change, Constitutional principles do not.

Points of Conflict

So what does the Constitution mean if we read it for its inherent principles? A few stand out as defining features from an Originalist perspective, especially *ordered liberty, collective rights*, and *federalism*. Ordered liberty was a core part of the Founders' vision for the constitutional order. Perhaps the best way to understand this principle is *balance*. The Constitution does not endorse an unrestrained democracy that follows the will of the people, nor does it endorse a system of absolute rights that allow for any type of individual behavior. Ordered liberty is a balance between democratic control and individual rights, without one dominating the other. This principle relies on the observation that the Bill of Rights is only a *part* of the Constitution, not the entire set of guiding principles (or even the primary ones). The document also establishes democratic control over the vast majority of public decisions not specifically affected by the limits of the Bill of Rights. It is more accurate to say that we have a republic limited by rights than a system of rights with a residual of democracy. Our rights are also intertwined with responsibilities; rights come with duties. In the current day those duties are not very large, but they still include decent conduct that at the very least does not harm others and maybe even does not degrade our society too much.

How do we know that the Constitution endorses this vision of ordered liberty and not pure liberty? The concept is clear in the beliefs and writings of the Founders, from Washington to Hamilton, and even Jefferson, but it is also inherent in the organization of the

Constitution. The Preamble offers a range of goals for the constitutional order, including promoting the general welfare and insuring domestic tranquility as well securing the blessings of liberty, suggesting a balance between different aspects of the system. The body of the Constitution reflects this same principle, focused primarily on collective decision-making by the people's representatives, but limited by the specific rights of individuals. Clearly there is intended to be a balance between local control and personal rights. Neither is designed to trump the other but rather to achieve balance, or the essence of ordered liberty.

The concept of balance is also reflected in the simultaneous protection of collective and individual rights. Personal rights that allow citizens to resist the control of the majority are an important part of our system, but so are the collective rights that allow the people to act as an organized body, controlling both tyrannical government and disruptive individuals. Originalism values the collective aspect of rights because they came first; the individual rights expanded by the Fourteenth Amendment are important but they did not eradicate the collective perspective that was already there. Instead they created a balance between the two.

Perhaps the strongest reflection of ordered liberty and collective rights is the constitutional principle of *federalism*. One of the clearest ways that ordered liberty can be achieved and collective rights can be asserted is through the local and state governments that have powers not afforded to the federal government. The police power—the traditional common law authority to regulate society for the safety, health, and morality of the community—is held by the states but *not* the federal government. The national government, on the other hand, faces specific structural limits designed to block its authority from expanding. While many contemporary thinkers see individual rights as the primary limit to government power (the government can act as long as it does not violate broad personal rights), the original design of the Constitution also protects citizens by limiting national authority. Both structural limits and rights protections work together to maintain liberty. For this reason, Originalists take seriously the limits imposed by the Interstate Commerce Clause. The federal government can regulate *interstate* trade that influences the entire nation, but not all aspects of the economy. The Commerce Clause is a meaningful limit rather than a blank check for federal power. The scope of the national economy has grown over the last two centuries along with our sense of national identity, but federalism remains a crucial part of the constitutional order.

Ordered liberty, collective rights, and federalism work in combination to ensure that the majority of our collective decisions are made through local democratic control. This explains the lesser regard that Originalists have for *judicial review*. Replacing democratic control with judicial oversight as a normal procedure was never the intent of the system. It is important to remember that the power of judicial review was seized by the Supreme Court rather than granted by the Constitution. Originalists take a similar view toward evolving *social facts*. Decisions about important changes in our society should be left to the normal democratic process rather than unelected Justices whenever possible. The principles of the Constitution clearly place the representation of the people before the beliefs of the Supreme Court Justices.

The Constitution also places a high value on the preservation of the Constitution. This may seem like an obvious statement, but not from the perspective of the other schools of thought. If we concentrate on contemporary beliefs and the expansion of individual rights, the preservation of the Constitution itself is not a prime concern. If we follow the explicit words of the document, it says nothing about its possible decline or dissolution. But the Founders believed that the new constitutional order was a fragile achievement ("a Republic, if you can keep it") and that its long-term survival was sincerely in doubt. If we take the fragility of the democratic system seriously, from both internal decline and foreign threat, then preservation may be the highest value of the Constitution. This explains why Originalism sees the military powers of the president as more expansive than the other schools of thought. When faced with military threats, other considerations must be subordinate. The United States Constitution does not survive if the United States itself does not survive. The Court once summarized this view in the statement that "the Constitution is not a suicide pact." If the circumstances dictate that any specific right endangers the whole constitutional order, then that right can be limited. When it comes to the possibility of transcendent values in the Constitution, Originalists are more likely to see preservation as the highest principle, coming before liberty in the list of priorities.

If we only concentrated on the explicit words of the document, or on their evolving meaning, or on the history of the precedents, we could easily miss the significance of fragility and preservation in the meaning of the Constitution. When reading the document we have to bring more of an understanding of the ideas and purposes behind it than just the text offers. This is why Textualism is not sufficient. The text alone does not explain the significance of the animating principles that the document upholds, including ordered liberty, separation of powers, unalienable rights, or federalism. In order to understand liberty, we have to see its purposes. In order to understand rights, we have to know what they are and how they came to us. In order to understand the Constitution, we have to inquire into its original meaning.

Weaknesses

Perhaps the greatest weakness of an Originalist approach is that it requires a broader knowledge of the Founding era in order to understand several of the principles of the Constitution. The start-up cost is higher, but Originalists argue that the payoff is much greater once those principles are understood. This is the core dispute between Originalists and Textualists, whether the document is fully complete on its own or loses important meaning without a grasp of the Founders' principles and the document's nuances. An example is the meaning of the Second Amendment.

Amendment II:　A well-regulated militia, being necessary to the security of a free state, the right of the people to keep and bear arms, shall not be infringed.

The language of the central clause is clear ("the right of the people to keep and bear arms shall not be infringed"), but the opening clause is not easy to follow on a first reading. Exactly what it means and how it affects the Amendment may not be understandable without recourse to more than just the plain meaning, which in this case is not plain at all. An Originalist would reflect on the meaning and purpose of the Amendment, especially what we can discern from the discussions surrounding its ratification and in the writings of the Founders.

Many contemporary readers insist that the Amendment is an anachronism in the current world given our concerns about gun violence.

Moreover, the text mentions the militia, which is no longer in force. But when we ask what the Framers believed was the purpose of the right, it takes on a different meaning: the Second Amendment ensures that an armed populace can assert and defend all of its rights against the possibility of a tyrannical government. The preceding clause of the Amendment is not a limit to this right, but a justification. The translation in contemporary American English of the eighteenth century "A well regulated militia being necessary to the security of a free state," is "*Because* a well-regulated militia *is* necessary to the security of a free state, the right to keep and bear arms shall not be infringed." This clause is a constitutional curiosity, because the document does not justify itself in other places. For example, the separation of powers into distinct branches of government is merely stated but not justified, nor is the right of free speech given its own reason, but the right to bear arms is. The justification of the Second Amendment is that when the government holds a monopoly of force, no rights are safe. The National Guard cannot be what the Amendment protects, because the Guard comprises only a fraction of the citizenry rather than the definition of the militia as all able-bodied men of the community. More importantly, *the National Guard is commanded by the government itself* and therefore cannot possibly usurp or replace the right recognized by the Second Amendment, which is directed *against* the government. While the ability to organize a militia is a collective right, it is grounded in the individual right to hold weapons, without which a militia or any other ability to protect oneself would not be possible. If we read the Constitution from the perspective of solving contemporary problems (as in the Common Law approach), or from the perspective of evolving social beliefs (as a Living Constitutionalist), we could be tempted to interpret the Second Amendment in a way the Framers did not intend. But beginning from its purpose and goal, its meaning is clear.

Seeking the original meaning of the Constitution leads to two standard criticisms: that we cannot recreate the Founders' world of the late eighteenth century, and that the Founders were not a unified group. The first is something of a red herring. We would only need to recreate the specific attitudes of the Founders if their premises were still the basis of contemporary decisions. But Originalists recognize that premises change over time. The Founders specific views of wiretaps or computers are not relevant because they didn't exist. Their understandings of women or minorities are also not relevant because those social facts have changed. What is relevant is their set of principles, which we apply to the new circumstances. Originalism is clear that premises can change even while principles do not.

The more interesting criticism is the potential disunity among the Founding generation. The original meaning could be difficult to discern if the Founders disagreed about it. If there are documented differences among the important members of the founding generation, how can we know the exact meaning? This criticism is often exaggerated by substituting the personal views of the various Founders for their understanding of the compromise that was reached among them. It is accurate to say that Adams, Hamilton, and Madison disagreed strenuously about what the Constitution *should* have said (if they alone had written it), but it is not accurate to say that they disagreed broadly about what it *does* say (after the agreements they reached). The final document represents a compromise among their various positions. Each provision of the document represents the best thinking of the Founders collectively, though not any one of them individually. As brilliant as several of them were independently, we can have much greater faith in their consensus views. Where a broad consensus was reached, on principles such as ordered liberty and federalism, we can have confidence in that interpretation. Small points of disagreement on the meaning of the document are not a block to understanding when it is broad agreement that illustrates constitutional principles.

Originalism places a high value on the consensus principles of the Founding era as expressed in the Constitution. In more recent decades our society has offered new ideas that challenge these principles in important ways. But Originalism does not accept the argument that new ideas, especially when held by only a part of our population, eradicate or replace our Founding beliefs. Constitutional principles do not simply alter automatically when contemporary citizens change their minds or attempt to redefine words. Our national principles can surely be changed by amendment, but not by the whim of the Justices. Reading the Constitution for its enduring meaning may create the best avenue for understanding.

14

LIVING CONSTITUTIONALISM

The newest of the four schools of interpretation emerged in the first half of the twentieth century in the time of the Progressive Era and the New Deal. But in its full form it is a product of the civil rights and social justice era of the 1960s, with its emphasis on the rights revolution in free speech, due process, and personal privacy as well as the rapid expansion of the role of women and minorities. In this tumultuous era of change, who could favor a dead Constitution? Living Constitutionalism is a great phrase, because its opposite is hard to advocate. I was taught as a kid that the Constitution evolves to fit the needs of our society as it changes, which means that of course it must be a living and not a dead document. Living Constitutionalism in this sense is often taught as the only reasonable or legitimate approach, but this masks the several different ways the term is applied.

There are at least three meanings of a Living Constitution. The first is that it recognizes important changes in our society to which we apply the Constitution. Everyone agrees with this, including Originalists, who do not deny that social norms and conditions change over time. This is not a school of thought because it does not stake out any unique territory, but is instead only a rhetorical device to suggest that because we know that change occurs, we must all be Living Constitutionalists.

The second meaning of a Living Constitution is a dismissal of the authority or majesty of the document, a rejection of its sacred or even core status as a defining feature of American society. In this view, the Constitution is old and in many ways no longer relevant to the contemporary world. In some ways it embodies the wrong values, but more importantly it blocks current political desires from being achieved. One of the early criticisms from the Living Constitutionalist perspective was that the original document is anti-democratic. *Readers Digest* published an article in 1931 with the title "Our Obsolete Constitution," arguing that we should "make our government at least as responsible, as flexible, as sensitive to public opinion as the parliamentary systems of Great Britain and the leading democracies of Europe."[63] One of those leading democracies was Germany, and the sensitivity of the German government to popular opinion during the 1930s allowed the fascist revolution that led to World War II, an example of the dangers of rampant democracy and committed popular movements that worried the Founders. The 1930s criticism of the Constitution as anti-democratic was eclipsed by the 1960s critique that it did not recognize individual rights *against* popular majorities, which became the focus of a Living Constitution as it is understood today.

Perhaps the most well-known contemporary critic of the Constitution was Thurgood Marshall. As Chief Counsel for the NAACP he argued many cases before the Supreme Court, including most famously the landmark desegregation case of *Brown v. Board of Education* in 1954. He was appointed to the Supreme Court a decade later by President Lyndon Johnson and, after his retirement in 1991, was replaced by Clarence Thomas. It is instructive to compare the two famous Marshalls of the Supreme Court. While John Marshall, the Chief Justice of *Marbury*, had a reverence for the Constitution, Thurgood Marshall did not see it in the same light. At the time of the bicentennial of the Constitution in 1987, he gave a famous speech that defines the critical aspect of Living Constitutionalism. It was later published in *The Howard Law Journal* under the title "The Constitution: A Living Document." Marshall argued that in the year of the bicentennial, "patriotic feelings will surely swell, prompting proud proclamations of the wisdom, foresight, and sense of justice shared by the Framers and reflected in a written document now yellowed with age. This is unfortunate—not the patriotism itself, but the tendency for the celebration to oversimplify, and overlook the many other events that have been instrumental to our achievements as a nation." In Marshall's view, the Constitution is not the wellspring of our nation's greatness, but instead it is the social movements and protests, especially of the 1960s and the civil rights era, that created what should be valued most. Marshall wrote that he cannot accept the invitation to praise the Constitution, "for I do not believe that the meaning of the Constitution was forever 'fixed' at the Philadelphia Convention. Nor do I find the wisdom, foresight, and sense of justice exhibited by the Framers particularly profound."[64] John Marshall saw the Framers as "enlightened patriots" and the Constitution as a sacred document of enduring principles, while Thurgood Marshall saw the Constitution as radically incomplete, not in the sense of needing information or details supplied by other aspects of the Founding era, but fundamentally lacking in principle as well as practice, which could only be supplied by later movements and ideas.

The third meaning of Living Constitutionalism is that the document's principles must change as we change. The meaning of the Constitution is not stable, but attached to the American people, and it is meant to alter as our principles evolve. The Supreme Court plays the central role in recognizing and implementing these changes when the time is right. This focus on evolving principles is the heart of Living Constitutionalism. While Originalists agree that premises change even if principles do not, Living Constitutionalists argue that *principles as well as premises change over time.*

How to Read the Constitution: Living Constitutionalism

If important principles change over time, then we must pay particular attention to evolving beliefs. The Constitution belongs to the American people and it is their interpretation that counts the most. In this sense the document is a vessel rather than a fixed message; it tells us to value liberty and equality, but how we understand those concepts is up to us and may not be at all as the Founders understood them. Living Constitutionalism values democracy, not in terms of local majorities getting their way, but in terms of a whole people changing how they view their core ideals, expanding them over time.

Perhaps the phrase that captures this ideal best is the "evolving standards of decency" of our society. The phrase originated in the case of *Trop v. Dulles* in 1958. *Trop* dealt with the Eighth Amendment prohibition against cruel and unusual punishment, but it was not a death penalty case. The constitutional question was whether the loss of citizenship for military desertion was cruel and unusual. Alan Trop was a natural born citizen who deserted from the U.S. Army in Casablanca during World War II. After his conviction at court-martial and completion of a sentence of three years at hard labor, he was dishonorably discharged from the military and stripped of his citizenship under the Nationality Act of 1940. In a controversial 5/4 decision, the Court ruled that imposing a condition of statelessness on a person in contemporary society was cruel and unusual, placing them in a permanent position of vulnerability. The Justices approached the question of the meaning of the Eighth Amendment from the perspective of what it had come to mean under current conditions, famously arguing that "the Amendment must draw its meaning from the evolving standards of decency that mark the progress of a maturing society."[65] When considering a Living Constitution, it is important to consider the new or emerging meaning of our principles, including liberty and equality as well as cruel and unusual punishment. The question is not what liberty *meant*, but what liberty *means*, not what the Constitution *protected*, but what it *protects*.

One of the clearest applications of Living Constitutionalism has been in the realm of criminal prosecution, especially the death penalty. Are state executions cruel and unusual, and how would we know? If the beliefs of our society shift over time, what is the standard for recognizing a change? One could argue that we now have access to very good information on public opinion through the regular polling of our citizens, so changes in our social values should be open to examination. But this raises the question of what sort of opinion we mean. Is it the average view of our citizens? Or is it the view of our more elite or educated citizens that should count? Or is it the future direction of our beliefs, what our society will come to believe rather than what it believes right now?

In *Furman v. Georgia*, the landmark decision that rejected the constitutionality of the death penalty in 1972, Thurgood Marshall argued in his concurring opinion that the death penalty "is morally unacceptable to the people of the United States at this time in their history."[66] However, he was not appealing to the normal views of our citizens. Marshall explicitly rejects the view that surveys or some other method of understanding the average citizen should be our goal, especially given that polling shows broad support for capital punishment by a substantial majority of our citizens. It is important to understand Marshall's reasoning in distinguishing between popular opinion and true American beliefs: "The question with which we must deal is not whether a substantial proportion of American citizens would today, if polled, opine that capital punishment is barbarously cruel, but whether they would find it to be so in the light of all information presently available ... a violation of the Eighth Amendment is totally dependent on the predictable subjective, emotional reactions of informed citizens."[67] In other words, the test is what citizens would believe *if they were fully informed*, not what they believe now. "I cannot believe that at this stage in our history, the American people would ever knowingly support purposeless vengeance. Thus, I believe that the great mass of citizens would conclude on the basis of the material already considered that the death penalty is immoral and therefore unconstitutional."[68] The important point in Marshall's view is not what the American people *have* concluded, but what they *would* conclude.

While Marshall's rejection of the death penalty was sweeping, the larger number of Justices in *Furman* rejected the death penalty on more limited grounds, and four years later the Court approved its reinstatement in *Gregg v. Georgia*, which instituted more stringent controls over the practice. Marshall dissented to that decision, arguing that

> The American people, fully informed as to the purposes of the death penalty and its liabilities, would in my view reject it as morally unacceptable. Since the decision in *Furman*, the legislatures of 35 States have enacted new statutes authorizing the imposition of the death sentence for certain crimes, and Congress has enacted a law providing the death penalty for air piracy resulting in death. I would be less than candid if I did not acknowledge that these developments have a significant bearing on a realistic assessment of the moral acceptability of the death penalty to the American people. But if the constitutionality of the death penalty turns, as I have urged, on the opinion of an informed citizenry, then even the enactment of new death statutes cannot be viewed as conclusive. In *Furman*, I observed that the American people are largely unaware of the information critical to a judgment on the morality of the death penalty, and concluded that if they were better informed they would consider it shocking, unjust, and unacceptable.[69]

The key factor is not what the American people profess to believe, but what they could or would believe in a more enlightened circumstance.

Reading the Constitution for what it has come to mean—or should mean—to our citizens requires an attention not only to changing circumstances but especially to the evolving values of our society.

Points of Conflict

Living Constitutionalism places a high value on the wisdom and judgment of the Justices of the Supreme Court. Marshall's view of the comparative value of the beliefs of normal citizens compared to the sentiments of more enlightened leaders is a clear statement of this perspective. If we are going to advance, we need leadership from the elites of our society, who must not hide behind mass opinion when it blocks us from the "more perfect union" that is our goal. Hence Living Constitutionalists depend on *judicial review* as a crucial facet of our democracy. The Constitution sets up a framework for a society of rights and human dignity, but did not provide the specific content to reflect that goal. It is significantly *incomplete*, requiring the addition of expanding rights grounded in the growing sensibilities of an educated populace.

If regard for judicial review is high and for the completeness of the Constitution is low, the Justices may need to recognize important trends even outside of the United States. In *Trop*, the Court argued that "the civilized nations of the world are in virtual unanimity that statelessness is not to be imposed as punishment for crime."[70] Forty-five years later in *Lawrence v. Texas* (the decision that declared the criminalization of homosexual behavior to be unconstitutional), the Justices again looked to foreign precedent as a guide. They referred to a recent decision of the European Court of Human Rights and invoked the "values we share with a wider civilization."[71]

In addition to *judicial review* and *completeness*, the third point of conflict that defines a Living Constitutionalist approach is *transcendence*. Again, *Lawrence* is a clear example. The ruling relies on a broad perception of liberty not found in any part or passage of the document, instead reflecting "the liberty of the person both in its spatial and more transcendent dimensions."[72] Transcendent liberty (or perhaps equality) allows the growing perceptions of personal rights to be incorporated into the meaning of the Constitution.

Just as Living Constitutionalism endorses expansive rights within the Constitution, it also advances the emerging *social facts* of our society. The first definition of Living Constitutionalism offered above—that it recognizes social change—suggests that those changes should be embraced quickly. In this sense a Living Constitutionalist approach goes beyond the agreement on this point from Originalists, who acquiesce to changes in social premises only after they have been clearly endorsed by the mainstream of society. Rather than waiting for a broad acceptance of new norms, Living Constitutionalists are willing to engage in the process of change and look ahead to the future of our society.

One way to summarize Living Constitutionalism is that it embraces the newer aspects of the points of conflict (transcendence, individual rights, and moving ahead of current social facts) and rejects the older ones (federalism, ordered liberty, and collective rights). Federalism is simply not as important as it was in the early days of the Republic before we became a unified nation. Similarly, ordered liberty is no longer the definition of freedom as we understand it. The incompleteness of the Constitution demands that we take into account the new ideas that our society offers, especially when core concepts like freedom are evolving in the direction of pure liberty. Collective rights are a fading concept compared to the growing—perhaps transcendent—individual rights that the Constitution has come to embody.

This growth and change in the Constitution has been influenced profoundly by the Fourteenth Amendment. When we read the document in a comprehensive and chronological way, an amendment can alter the meaning of the earlier text. But no amendment has had broader influence than the Fourteenth. For Living Constitutionalism, this amendment is a cornerstone of the new Constitutional order, changing the original document in four major ways:

1. It *applies the Bill of Rights to the states*, expanding their protections to all levels of government power.
2. It shifts the nature of rights to an *individual rather than collective* foundation; all of the protections of the Bill of Rights now reside in individual citizens, eradicating the collective rights tradition that served as the foundation for ordered liberty.
3. It rewrote the Tenth Amendment and its principle of federalism. In a post-Fourteenth Amendment America—in which rights are grounded in individuals and the balance of power has shifted to

the national level—*federalism in no longer a guiding principle*. In essence the Tenth Amendment has been written out of the Constitution.

4. It added *equality* as a key constitutional principle, as embodied in the Equal Protection Clause. In order to achieve this new goal, the federal government has greater powers through the Commerce Clause and the Necessary and Proper Clause of Article I. Each of these clauses in their original form empowered the Congress to act in a limited fashion, but these powers are expanded when read through the lens of the Fourteenth. At this point in the development of our nation, one of the key sources of the denial or achievement of equality is employment in commercial enterprise, as addressed through the Commerce Clause. The Necessary and Proper Clause grants broad authority "for carrying into execution the foregoing powers, and all other powers vested by this Constitution in the government of the United States," which includes the new concerns with equality.

Figure 14.1 details the expansive influence of the Fourteenth Amendment in the view of Living Constitutionalists. Well beyond its influence on the Bill of Rights, the amendment increases the powers of the federal government in Article I and decreases the role of federalism found in the Tenth Amendment. The focus of the Fourteenth Amendment and the Bill of Rights on individual rights and equality replaces the original document's emphasis on federalism and ordered liberty as foundations of the Constitutional order.

Weaknesses

Perhaps the greatest criticism leveled at Living Constitutionalism is that it is standardless. If the Justices are not tied to the text, or framed by the Founding, or bound to the precedents, then they are free to see in the Constitution their own political desires. Judging the future values of our society may be the same thing as creating those future values. Living Constitutionalism requires great trust in the wisdom of unelected and irremovable Justices, which may be a great deal to ask.

Living Constitutionalism also assumes that change is good (that contemporary ideas are better than the Founding ones, the opposite assumption of Originalism). The goal is to identify the evolving

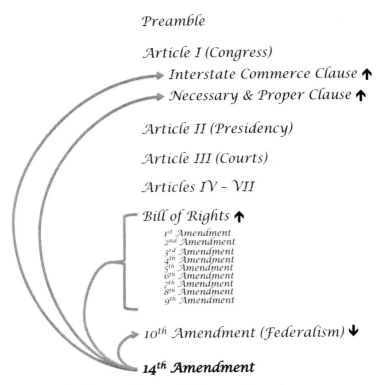

Figure 14.1 The Expansive Influence of the Fourteenth Amendment

standards of decency of a maturing society. But it may be hard to tell a maturing society from a rotting society; the new standards could reflect either one. The Justices wield great power in this approach. They can create new doctrines like substantive due process, fundamental rights, or personal privacy. They can also ignore established doctrines like the gun rights of the Second Amendment or the federalist principle of the Tenth. This takes us back to the original point that Living Constitutionalism is open to the charge of being unprincipled and opportunistic. A Living Constitution may be no Constitution at all. Being able to throw out any part of the Constitution you don't like makes it hard to defend the parts you do. On the other hand, being tied to an inflexible document may not allow society to progress.

15

COMPARING SCHOOLS
OF INTERPRETATION

We have four distinct ways of reading the Constitution: it means what it says; it means what the Supreme Court has said it says; it means what the Founders thought it says; or it means what we have come to believe it says. Before you decide which of these approaches makes the most sense, there are a few final comparisons to take into consideration.

Points of Conflict

Perhaps the clearest guide to the schools of thought is your set of reactions to the nine points of conflict discussed in Part I. The figures below demonstrate how the points of conflict line up against each of the schools of interpretation, illustrating many of the relationships we have discussed. It may be useful to plot out your initial inclinations on each of the conflicts in order to see which school this indicates. Figure 15.1 compares the positions on *judicial review* and the *completeness* of the Constitution. If the document is by its nature incomplete and judicial review is a necessary feature of our system to fill in those gaps, this leads to a Living Constitutionalist or Common Law approach. Living Constitutionalists see the incompleteness being handled by contemporary values while Common Law thinkers see the answer in past precedents and new workable rules, but both turn to judicial review as the heart of the system. Textualists reject both of these arguments, taking the strongest position that the document is complete, even perfect, and rejecting judicial review whenever possible in favor of political representation through elections. Originalists move away from the purity of the Textualist position, seeing a slightly broader role

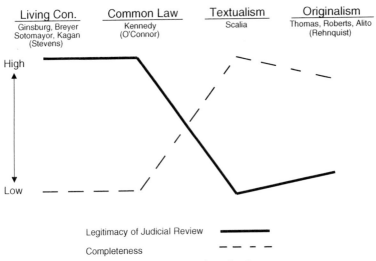

Figure 15.1 Schools of Thought and Points of Conflict I

of judicial review and especially a need for an understanding of the Founding era in order to interpret the Constitution.

Figure 15.2 displays the core points of conflict that move together from low to high as we travel from the left to the right on the spectrum of constitutional interpretation. *Ordered liberty, collective rights,* and *federalism* all work in concert. Ordered liberty as an ideal is supported by collective rights and the local control provided by federalism. The federalist principle has several purposes including avoiding tyranny and allowing for regional differences, but also reinforcing ordered liberty at the local level. To Living Constitutionalists all of these ideals are anachronisms that are dead or deserve to be; to Common Law Constitutionalists they have some resonance in the precedents; to Textualists they are indicated in the document itself; and to Originalists they are clear principles of the Founders. The same is true of *religion* as a foundation of the constitutional order: Living Constitutionalism rejects it most firmly in the contemporary world, while Orginalism accepts that whether one is religious or not in private life, it is one of the foundations of our system, explaining the origin of immutable rights and the source of a stable society.

The final figure displays the points of conflict that have more complex relationships to the schools of thought. *Transcendence*—the

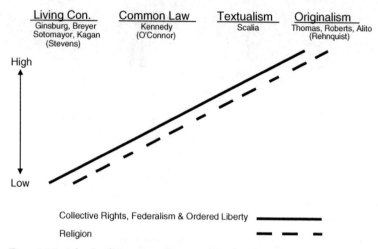

Figure 15.2 Schools of Thought and Points of Conflict II

perception that when read as a whole the Constitution recognizes broad principles or rights that must be upheld—is associated with Living Constitutionalism and falls to its low point as we move to Textualism, which has the strongest disagreement with that perspective. Interestingly, transcendence ticks up once again as we move to Originalism due to its regard for preservationist transcendence. Many Originalists see preservation as a transcendent value above the explicit provisions of the document, which reinforces a strong regard for executive power in the face of threats, a clear disagreement with Textualists. Transcendent Originalism is not the same sort of contradiction that transcendent Textualism would be. One way of understanding the original meaning of the Constitution is that it created a set of transcendent commitments that resonate throughout the document, beginning with preservation and moving to ordered liberty, federalism, religion, and collective rights.

Precedent displays an inverted U-curve in relation to the schools of thought, lowest at the ends and highest in the middle. A high regard for following precedent leads to a Common Law view, while valuing the correct interpretation more than the precedents corresponds with Living Constitutionalism on the left and either Textualism or Originalism on the right. The final point of conflict, the evolution of *social facts*, plays a large role in both Living Constitutionalist and Common

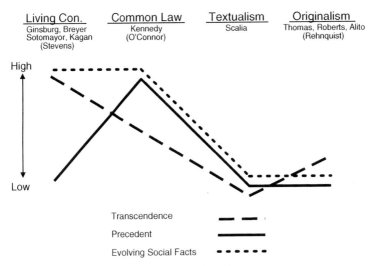

Figure 15.3 Schools of Thought and Points of Conflict III

Law thinking, allowing the Justices of the Court to determine what changes have taken place and how best to react to them. Textualists and Originalists take a dimmer view of the role of the Justices in discerning and especially of moving ahead of society's current social premises, instead leaving these decisions in the hands of the representative process as much as possible.

Comparisons

A few final questions remain about the competing approaches. These are illustrated in Table 15.1 and can be used to test your thoughts on which school of interpretation is most persuasive. The first question is *what are the most important and least important parts of the Constitution?* The schools of thought take very different views of what truly counts as well as what can be safely ignored. To a Living Constitutionalist, the most important part of the Constitution is clearly the Bill of Rights. This aspect of the document explains the expansive individual rights at the core of American beliefs. The Amendments are the mechanisms that allow us to adapt to changing circumstances and add new beliefs to the system. The Fourteenth Amendment may be even more important than the original Bill of Rights, because it individualized the previous rights and nationalized our perspective on government. Originalists, on the other hand, see it as odd that additions to a document would be considered more important than the document itself. The core of the Constitution is clearly Article I, which was first in the Framers' minds and sets up the most important facet of our government—a system of representation to decide our public questions. The heart of the Constitution is a republican democracy carried out through elections, not a judicial democracy undertaken by Supreme Court Justices. To Common Law Constitutionalists, the most important part of the document is Article III, which sets up the Supreme Court and the judicial system that allows Justices to craft the doctrines and precedents that are the bedrock of the Constitution. For Textualists, the most important part of the document is an impossible question, because all of the text is equally significant.

If these are the most important parts of the Constitution, what are the least important? For Living Constitutionalists, it is likely the Second Amendment or maybe the Tenth. Both are remnants of a previous era, on the one hand upholding gun rights in the wilderness and on the other hand privileging local rights before we became a national entity. Neither reflects the contemporary world. The least important to Originalists is Article III, as the Justices have the least power and role in our system (the mirror image of the Common Law perspective). Textualists on principle should see nothing as less important, just as they see nothing in particular as the most important part. But in practice, the least important facet of the document is the Ninth Amendment. Its text provides no specific content, so Textualists tend to rate it as insignificant. The least important part from a Common Law perspective is more difficult to say. It may be the aspects of the document that have been neglected or effectively eradicated by the precedents of the Court, including the Privileges and Immunities Clause of the Fourteenth Amendment. The Court's early refusal to follow this part of the amendment led to the creation of the fundamental rights doctrine, which is accepted by Common Law thinkers as a part of the constitutional canon, while being highly suspect to Textualists and Originalists.

The next question in Table 15.1 is *What evolves?* To Originalists, premises evolve but principles do not, while Living Constitutionalists see both principles and premises as evolving in meaningful ways. To

Table 15.1 Comparing Schools of Interpretation

	Living Constitution	Common Law	Textualism	Originalism
Most Important Part of the Constitution?	Bill of Rights 14th Amendment	Article III	All	Article I
Least Important?	2nd Amendment 10th Amendment	Privileges & Immunities Clause	9th Amendment	Article III
What Evolves?	Principles & Premises	Precedents	Nothing Important	Premises but not Principles
Who Is Trusted?	Justices' Values	Justices' Reasoning	Founders' Language	Founders' Principles
Who Is the Smartest Person in the Room?	Justices (know the right values)	Justices (know the clever answer)	Constitution	Framers
Achilles' Heel?	Consistent Principle	Legitimacy of New Workable Rules	Meaning of the 9th Amendment	Understanding the Founders

Common Law thinkers, the most important evolution is the precedents of the Supreme Court. But to Textualists, the clearest answer is nothing that we should be concerned about. The text does not evolve at all (unless changed officially by Amendment) and the evolution of social facts is the province of legislatures rather than Court, which makes the Justices' role simply one of recognizing these manifest changes once they have occurred. What evolves from the perspective of each approach is no small question, with four distinct answers: nothing important, everything that counts, the precedents, or the premises but not the principles.

Another way to distinguish among the schools of interpretation is to ask *whom do they trust*? Originalism trusts legislatures to get it right most of the time, but at the core of Originalism is a trust of the Founders' principles, which are the most important guide to a free and decent society. Textualists take a similar view, but trust more in the Founders' explicit words than in interpretations of their principles.

Common Law thinkers trust in the reasoning capacity of the Justices, both past and present, to develop clear and consistent rules that handle the complexity of modern society. And Living Constitutionalists place the greatest trust in the value systems of the Justices to guide wise decisions.

If we phrase the question in the reverse—*who is not trusted?*—this also tells us important things. Living Constitutionalists do not quite trust the Founders' principles, or at least find them suspect, out of date, too elitist, possibly racist, possibly sexist, and clearly restrictive of contemporary desires for change. Nor do they trust state legislatures or local governments, who may well trample the rights of individuals, especially ones who do not fit in with the group. Textualists and Originalists do not trust Justices, who will force their own values and perceptions into the document rather than follow what it truly says or means.

One of my favorite questions that I believe clarifies the competing approaches is *Who is the smartest person in the room?* For Living Constitutionalists and Common Law thinkers it is the most intellectual Justices, who have the insight into the right values or the cleverness to craft the right solution. For Originalists it is always the Founders, not any living person who claims to have better ideas than Adams, Franklin, Hamilton, Jefferson, Madison, and Washington did. For Textualists, the document itself is always the greatest source of wisdom in the room, what the Framers wrote rather than what we believe they thought.

The final question we should ask is the Achilles' heel of each approach. It is fitting to end this way because none of the perspectives is without criticism. It is important to weigh their flaws against each other, as well as to ask how they can be minimized or overcome. The most noted flaw of Textualism is that in many cases the Constitution does not give clear guidance through the explicit text alone. Most Textualists admit this and default to Originalism to fill in those blanks when the text is not sufficient. Their argument is that the text should come first and only when necessary should we inquire into the original meaning. Another Textualist answer to this criticism is that ambiguity is not really a problem; it is instead a command to *not* act. Whenever the text is unclear, the Supreme Court should allow the normal democratic process to unfold. Only when the text is clear are the Justices authorized to intervene. Perhaps the larger problem for a Textualist approach is the role of the Ninth Amendment. Because it gives no specific indication of which rights are reserved to the people, Textualists tend to conclude it is merely symbolic, with no literal meaning. But this violates the convention of reading the Constitution as if it were written carefully and every part has a purpose. So it has to mean something, yet to a Textualist it can't mean anything. One way out of this dilemma is the argument that the Ninth Amendment refers to *rights of long usage*. These are the primordial rights that citizens have been exercising from before the time of the Founding, including holding property and traveling at will, as well as many of the rights recognized in other amendments such as holding weapons or associating with other citizens. In this interpretation the Ninth Amendment is not meaningless, but neither is it a wellspring of new or created rights.

The Achilles' heel of the Common Law approach is the origin of the new workable rules that are at the heart of this school of thought. They have no basis in the Constitution itself, but instead come only from the minds of the Justices. Their legitimacy as *constitutional* rules is questionable, as is their entrenchment as fixed precedents. This is especially the case if they turn out to not be as workable as their creators had envisioned. An over-reliance on precedent is another potential flaw. Sometimes the earlier decisions of the Court are simply wrong and an overburdening reliance on precedent can merely prolong the errors.

The flaw of Originalism is that the original meaning is itself open to a degree of interpretation, requiring a deep understanding of the ideas of the founding generation. The possible disagreements among the Founders increase this difficulty. Living Constitutionalists see this approach as being nearly as interpretive as their own, though Originalists respond that they have a standard—the historical record, which we can all examine—rather than merely the personal interpretations or desires of contemporary Justices. Living Constitutionalism allows for the expansion and re-interpretation of the Constitution to meet current needs, but this is its flaw as well as its virtue: how can we have consistent principle or predictable law when it is open to the whim of the Justices? A written Constitution means little if it can be changed through nothing more than finding a new right buried in the Due Process Clause or deciding that an established right is no longer necessary.

Each school of thought has its flaws, but we must choose an approach regardless. It is no excuse that no means of interpretation is perfect. An imperfect approach is all we have for understanding our system of government. The means do not match the importance of the task, so our own effort must make up the difference.

16

POINTS OF CONFLICT AND
SCHOOLS OF THOUGHT
IN A LANDMARK CASE

Roe v. Wade

One of the most important and most disputed constitutional cases of
the past fifty years is *Roe v. Wade*, the landmark decision that ended
the legal restriction of abortion in the United States. At the time of *Roe*
in 1973, abortion was illegal in most states, with a few exceptions such
as New York, Alaska, Hawaii, and Washington. Overturning those
laws placed abortion at the center of our legal and political battles of
the last forty years.

It would be difficult to write an explanation of our constitutional
conflicts without addressing the *Roe* decision and the intense disputes
over the meaning of the Constitution that it invokes. The ruling not
only reflects intense moral disagreement, but also illustrates several of
the core divisions over how to read the Constitution.

The chart below gives us a clear way of illustrating the important
aspects of the case. The nine points of conflict are listed vertically,
in the same order they are discussed in the book. The four schools of
thought are arrayed horizontally, from ideological left to right. Each
element that drives the decision is displayed in bold. This system can
be used to illustrate the dynamics of any given constitutional case,
highlighting its most important aspects. Normally a few points of
conflict and one school of thought are the key elements of any given
dispute, but in *Roe* it is important to note that the case deals with
the majority of the points of conflict and invokes two of the major
schools of interpretation, relying on the core arguments of Living
Constitutionalism in one sense and Common Law Constitutionalism
in another. One reason for the enduring controversy about the decision
is the sheer number of different disagreements on which it takes a

strong position. Depending on your perspectives on the conflicts we have discussed, there is a great deal to like or to dislike.

Judicial Review
Individual Versus Collective Rights
Federalism
Ordered Liberty
Religion
Transcendence
Premises
Precedent
Completeness

Living	**Common**	Textualism	Originalism
Constitutionalism	**Law**		

The facts of the case are relatively straightforward. Norma McCorvey, a twenty-one-year-old unmarried woman with a ninth-grade education, became aware of her third unintentional pregnancy.[73] She sought an abortion but was unable to find a willing doctor under the laws of the state of Texas. Her case took much longer than nine months to reach the Supreme Court, so by the time of the decision, McCorvey (known as Jane Roe in the case file) had already put the child up for adoption, but the constitutional question remained: can a state outlaw abortion without violating protections found in the Constitution, specifically privacy rights?

The Supreme Court said *No*, with seven Justices in the majority and two dissenters. In order to fully understand what was decided in *Roe*, it is important to identify the distinct aspects of the ruling:

1. Privacy is a fundamental right, grounded in the Due Process Clause of the Fourteenth Amendment.
2. Privacy encompasses the right to an abortion, which is a private act.
3. This is not an absolute right, because a government interest in fetal life grows during the term of pregnancy, until something approaching personhood develops near the beginning of the third trimester at the point of viability, when a newborn could survive on its own outside the mother.

4. Prior to this point, a fetus is not a person and does not have rights during the early stages of pregnancy.

Principles

The most well-known part of the decision is the ruling on constitutional principle: *privacy is a fundamental right.* The Court had upheld a constitutional right to privacy in earlier cases dealing with contraception, especially *Griswold v. Connecticut* in 1965, but had not recognized it as fundamental. So what is *privacy* as opposed to *liberty*? *Roe* shies away from giving a specific definition of privacy, instead arguing that surely it includes personal choices about procreation ("the right of privacy, however based, is broad enough to cover the abortion decision").[74] The Court has never offered an explicit definition, but the aspects of life it protects—contraception, child-rearing, and the sanctity of the home—give it more clarity.[75] In a sense, privacy is broader than the specific protections of individual liberty found in the Bill of Rights, but, in another sense, privacy is more exact in that it deals with intimate personal decisions that have no relation to other people. Privacy is protected specifically because it affects no one else, unlike individual liberties like free speech that may well influence other citizens in public. Privacy relates to actions that others have no reasonable means of even being aware of or noticing.

What sets *Roe* apart from the previous decisions that recognized a privacy right is the elevation of the right to fundamental status. In chapter 3 we discussed the emergence of the fundamental rights doctrine and the controversy over the discretion that it grants Justices to decide what is and is not given the highest level of constitutional protection. Fundamental rights are those that are held to be "intrinsic to a scheme of ordered liberty," meaning that the constitutional order would be meaningfully damaged or compromised if the liberty were not upheld. Under the fundamental rights doctrine as developed in the Court's previous rulings, the most important rights can only be infringed if the government has a "compelling state interest." This means that the government has no choice due to overriding circumstances but to undertake the action against the individual and no other means that would accomplish the same end. This standard is known as applying *strict scrutiny*. The Supreme Court has rarely found that

Table 16.1 The Fundamental Rights Doctrine

	Standard	Requirement	Meaning
Fundamental Right:	Strict Scrutiny	Compelling State Interest	1) the government must take the action 2) less-restrictive means are not available
Liberty Interest:	Rational Basis Test	Rational Basis	1) the government has a good reason 2) a non-arbitrary standard is employed

this standard is met, outside of pressing emergencies invoking national security. Claims to liberty that do not invoke a fundamental right only require a *rational basis*, which means simply that the government has a legitimate reason and applies the legal standard to everyone equally without singling out specific individuals. The result of this separation into two categories is that strict scrutiny is almost impossible to pass and a rational basis is difficult to fail. Once a right is deemed to be fundamental, government actions are severely limited.

Perhaps even more controversial than whether privacy is fundamental is its foundation in the Constitution. The great question of principle in *Roe* is *Where is the privacy right in the Constitution?* The Court retreated from the *Griswold* doctrine of penumbras, or a near-transcendent perception of privacy residing throughout the Bill of Rights. The Court also avoided the argument that privacy is a right found under the broad but unspecific protections of the Ninth Amendment. Instead the Court focused on the Fourteenth Amendment, finding a right of individual privacy in the Due Process Clause. According to *Roe*, privacy is inherent in the notion of protection against arbitrary state action. Privacy is not transcendent, but is invoked by the Fourteenth Amendment vision of individual liberty. This is the core of the ruling on constitutional principle.

Premises

The ruling on premises is if anything even more controversial. In the four-point rendition of *Roe* given above, the definition of a fetus comes last, but it may well have come first given that the decision recognizes with clarity that a different ruling would have made all discussion of privacy considerations irrelevant: many citizens "argue that the fetus is a 'person' within the language and meaning of the Fourteenth Amendment ... If this suggestion of personhood is established, the appellant's case, of course, collapses, for the fetus' right to life would then be guaranteed specifically by the Amendment. The appellant conceded as much on reargument."[76] Because the Fourteenth Amendment guarantees that life, liberty, or property cannot be taken without due process of law, a voluntary act by a private citizen depriving another person of life cannot be allowed. In an important sense, the heart of the decision and the new finding of *Roe* was less the principle and more the premise. The right of privacy had been established in previous rulings and was extended in *Roe* to include the abortion decision. The new ruling that allowed this extension was the premise that a fetus is not a person.

The grounds offered for the central premise revolve around the question of dependence, or whether a fetus is an independent entity. The decision offers a historical summary illustrating the variability in the interpretation of a fetus in the eyes of different authorities and traditions, including the ancient Greeks, the common law, Catholic and other theologies, and expert groups such as the American Medical Association. The Court concludes that in many interpretations "the fetus was to be regarded as part of the mother, and its destruction, therefore, was not homicide."[77]

While the Court takes a clear stance on this social premise, the decision also questions the ability of the Justices to offer a definitive position: "When those trained in the respective disciplines of medicine, philosophy, and theology are unable to arrive at any consensus, the judiciary, at this point in the development of man's knowledge, is not in a position as to answer." Nonetheless they do so, ruling that "the word 'person,' as used in the Fourteenth Amendment, does not include the unborn."[78] If the sentiment about the limits of the Court's knowledge is taken seriously, the alternative is to let our normal representative politics decide the question grounded in the views of our citizens. This brings us back to the question of how the Court should decide premises that are not addressed in the text of the Constitution. Should the Justices use their discretion to decide the current state of our social premises? Or should they defer to the judgments of our legislatures and allow majority rule through democratic representation to make those decisions? The Court takes the position in *Roe* that the Justices are in the best position to make the call.

The ruling is also clear that even though a fetus is not a person at the beginning of a pregnancy, its personhood and therefore a compelling state interest in its life grows over time. The critical question is when this point is reached and the Court establishes *viability* as the answer. This standard is offered without much discussion or justification, perhaps because of its clear connection with independence.[79] The process occurs for each fetus during the nine month gestation, crossing the threshold from dependence to independence—hence into personhood—at the point of viability. What the Court is really saying when its positions are added together is that 1) a fetus is not a person when conceived, 2) at some point the fetus becomes a person, and 3) we cannot identify that point with precision, but viability is the best available standard.

A second premise ruling, less-noted but also critical to the decision, revolves around the nature of abortion itself, specifically that it is a private and not a public act. Rights to privacy attach only to acts that are essentially private in character. But unlike other actions the Court has placed under the umbrella of privacy by virtue of their intimacy between two independent citizens, abortion encompasses medical professionals within a more public setting. Given the participation of a third party, who is a member a profession that comes under the regulation of the government, it is less clear that abortion is only a private act. Privacy rights in previous cases applied to situations in which citizens are alone in their decisions and actions, with no organs of the state or eyes of other citizens. This is why the bedroom is the quintessential example of a realm of privacy, because it involves only two people, generally speaking, away from the vision of society. Medicine, however, is a regulated profession that occurs outside of the bedroom. Of course, medical procedures are not a *public* act either, but there are not merely two categories of fully private or fully public, because many situations contain elements of each. Privacy rights as they have been described in the past only protect *purely* private acts; mixed acts and fully public ones are not protected (any public aspect means that an act is no longer private). The Court in *Roe* makes the ruling that abortion falls under the category of a private act with less justification than for the premise ruling on fetuses, leaving it potentially more vulnerable.

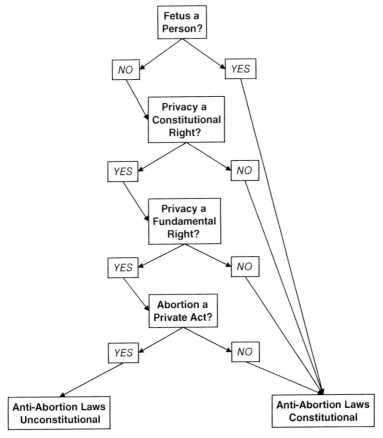

Figure 16.1 Decision Points in *Roe v. Wade*

Figure 16.1 illustrates the critical decision points in the case. The first is a premise question (*Is a fetus a person?*). The next two are questions of principle (*Is privacy a constitutional right?* and *Is that right fundamental?*). The final decision is again a question of premise (*Is abortion a private act?*). Answers of No, Yes, Yes, and Yes lead to the conclusion that abortion laws are unconstitutional; any other configuration of answers leads to the conclusion that they are not forbidden under the Constitution and remain a matter of individual state laws.

This is a great deal of decision making, but the ruling does not stop there. The final aspect of *Roe* is the trimester framework that clarifies the ability of the government to regulate abortion. Under *Roe*'s premises, a fetus is not a person at the beginning of a pregnancy, but its personhood grows over time. The decision offers a framework grounded in the medical terminology of trimesters (the first three months of pregnancy, the second three months, and the final three months). The government cannot ban or regulate abortion during the first trimester. During the second, the state cannot ban but can regulate the procedure for the safety and health of the mother. And during the third trimester (approximating viability) the government can ban abortion altogether. This system reflects the ruling's specific principles (regarding privacy) and its premises (regarding a fetus and abortion), combined with the judgment of the Justices about how these considerations interact with current medical practices. There is a great deal going on in *Roe*, which is as complex as it is important, but we can clarify it by concentrating on the points of conflict and schools of interpretation that it invokes.

Points of Conflict

Roe takes a position on at least six of the nine points of constitutional conflict that we have identified. The decision implicitly endorses a positive approach to *judicial review*, accepting a broad role for the Justices to rule on social controversies. It is important to remember that the Supreme Court does not have to take any given case, allowing them to easily sidestep a public issue and leave it in the hands of the democratic process. If they believe a case involves an unavoidable constitutional question, they can address that question in the most limited fashion available rather than undertake a full review of several elements of the controversy and announce a newly crafted legal standard as the Court does in *Roe*.

In regard to the point of conflict over the *nature of rights*, the decision in *Roe* reflects the perception that individual rather than collective rights are the basis of the Constitutional order, grounded in the influence of the Fourteenth Amendment. The ruling not only locates the right of privacy in the Due Process Clause of the Fourteenth, but also embraces the fundamental rights doctrine, increasing judicial discretion along with the expansion of individual rights.

The third conflict on which *Roe* takes a strong position is *federalism*, this time on the negative side. It rejects the Federalist claim that the individual states should be able to decide their own standards, instead focusing on the aspects of the Constitution that invoke individual rights that can travel throughout the union and create one national standard.

Roe takes an equally negative position on *ordered liberty*. The decision rejects the traditional power of local governments to regulate for moral purposes, replacing this power with the contemporary vision of pure liberty that disentangles rights from responsibilities and provides individuals with a broader range of free choice regardless of the views of the community. Similarly, the *religious* foundations of the constitutional order are implicitly rejected in favor of secular traditions, especially in considering the core premise ruling on the nature of a fetus.

One of the strongest positions influencing the decision is a positive view of the Court's role in determining *social facts*. The Justices undertook the burden of ruling upon the nature of a fetus rather than leaving that determination to our elected branches. The more significant question is the standard for that finding, whether the Court should attempt to judge the current view of society or move ahead of the current social norm, influencing rather than reflecting the prevalent social premise. Where the mainstream of our society is on any particular premise at any specific time is difficult to determine, but I believe it is likely that in 1973 the judgment that a fetus was not a person was moving ahead of American society. In the current day we may have reversed this sentiment, with a broad segment of our society accepting the view that a fetus is not yet a person, though there are significant parts of our population who clearly do not agree. Has the increasing movement toward the Court's view been an independent shift, or did *Roe* itself encourage that change in perspective? This is a difficult question that reflects the controversy over the role of the Justices in determining social premises.

Schools of Thought

Roe clearly illustrates the differences among the schools of interpretation over how to read the Constitution. If we follow the approach suggested above and illustrated in Figures 15.1 to 15.3, comparing the positions on the points of conflict to the schools of interpretation, *Roe* leaves little question of the dominant approach it takes. A positive position on judicial review, negative on collective rights, federalism, ordered liberty, and religion, and positive on social facts all align directly with Living Constitutionalism. The argument in *Roe* clearly reflects this perspective. The recognition of a non-textual right of privacy is one of the major additions of Living Constitutionalism to the body of constitutional law in the twentieth century. The decision argues that we have come to believe in this right as society has evolved. Though not discussed in the document itself, it is there nonetheless because of the evolution of our society toward accepting this broad definition of liberty. The first paragraphs of the decision invoke the changing circumstances of modern society ("population growth, pollution, poverty, and racial overtones tend to complicate and not simplify the problem").[80] The longest section of the decision is Part VI, which discusses at length the history of abortion law in the Western world and the evolving attitudes of several social organizations, including the American Medical Association and the American Public Health Association, as well as the American Bar Association. The opinions of doctors, public health practitioners, and lawyers were offered to illustrate the increasing acceptance of the view that a fetus is not a person. In both principle and premise, the key is the evolution of our society.

The Living Constitutionalist reasoning is paired with a Common Law result—the trimester framework. In order to reconcile the several aspects of individual privacy rights and growing personhood over the course of a pregnancy, the Court applies a new rule, crafted by Justice Blackmun after long discussion with legal and medical professionals. It is designed to be workable, presenting a practical standard by which individual citizens can understand what rights they do and do not have while state legislatures can understand what they can and cannot regulate. However, the viability standard has been criticized because it is dependent on the state of medicine at any given time. The point of viability is likely to be earlier with each passing decade as our medical knowledge and technology improves.

The combination of Living Constitutionalism and Common Law Constitutionalism explains why *Roe* is so disliked by Textualists and Originalists. It offers the most problematic elements of each approach, recognizing a non-textual constitutional right and creating a new Common Law standard to make it workable. Both of these approaches increase the power of the Justices at the expense of democratic representation. The heart of *Roe* is the creation of a right not found in either the text or original meaning of the Constitution and raising this right to fundamental status through the judgment of the Justices, stripping citizens of the ability to decide the issue or determine the prevailing social premise regarding a fetus. In one of the many cases dealing with abortion regulation following the *Roe* decision, Scalia wrote that "the permissibility of abortion, and the limitations upon it, are to be resolved like most important questions in our democracy: by citizens trying to persuade one another and then voting."[81]

One way to illustrate the clashing perspectives of the schools of thought is to return to Figure 16.1 and the four decision points of *Roe*. We can see clearly how each school of interpretation would respond to the questions presented. To the first question of our social premise regarding the nature of a fetus, Living Constitutionalism would move ahead of society; the answer to whether a fetus is a person is *No*. A Common Law approach could go either way if this were the first time the question were in front of the Court depending on the judgment of the Justices regarding the current conditions of society and its needs, but in the current day the precedents clearly indicate that a fetus is not a person. Both Textualism and Originalism would leave the question to the democratic process, which in this case seemed to say *Yes*, though either approach would likely focus on other aspects of the case before reaching the question of personhood.

To the second question, regarding the existence of a constitutional right to privacy, a Living Constitutionalist approach would clearly say *Yes*. To answer this question from a Common Law perspective we would have to specify whether we meant now or at the time of *Roe*. At that time a Common Law thinker would likely have agreed with the Living Constitutionalists given the needs of our society regarding poverty, crime, teenage pregnancy, and the increasing need for women to control their own fertility decisions in order to participate in society. At the current day, there is no question but that the precedents insist that a right to privacy exists. Textualists would adamantly say *No* grounded in the lack of textual support, while Originalists would reach a similar position given that the concept of privacy stretches the clear meaning of the liberties invoked by the Constitution and violates the general intent of democratic control of these decisions.

On the subsequent question of whether privacy rights are fundamental, Originalists and Textualists would reject the entire notion, given that privacy is not any kind of constitutional right, and even if it were, the fundamental rights doctrine is a vaguely illegitimate judicial invention that seizes far too much discretion for the Justices. Living Constitutionalists would say *Yes*, and Common Law thinkers would likely agree in the first instance and would definitely agree now given the dominant precedents.

For the final question—is abortion a private act?—the answers are again quite different. Living Constitutionalism would argue that it must be considered private in order to increase the range of individual liberties, especially given that our society has been moving in the direction of increasing realms of privacy that should encompass any medical procedure. Again, Common Law thinking is unpredictable if this were the first time the question had been raised, but the answer offered by the precedents is clearly *Yes*. Textualism would see this as an illegitimate judicial question. The Justices have no way to know, and, moreover, it is not relevant since there is no constitutional right of privacy; it is a manufactured question based on a manufactured right. Originalists would tend to agree, leaving such decisions in the hands of the public if they had to be answered.

Living Constitutionalism supports privacy rights because it concentrates on how society has or will evolve and emphasizes the role of the Justices in recognizing these important changes. The Constitution must be read with these changing social values and circumstances in mind. The Common Law approach supports the trimester framework because it emphasizes the importance of Justices taking a lead role in crafting workable solutions to contemporary problems, following and building upon the precedents of the Supreme Court as a way of understanding the Constitution. Both of these approaches oppose the Textualist view that the document must be read only as it is written, which would not allow for the insistence on privacy rights that the Constitution does not include, nor for the creation of new Common Law standards that the Justices have no business crafting. The *Roe* decision also violates several of the core perceptions of Originalism, including a respect for federalism, for ordered liberty, and for collective rights, all of which argue that state governments have a more expansive power to regulate society. The meaning of the principles inherent in the document simply do not include a right of individual privacy as broad as the one recognized in *Roe*; society can decide to allow access to abortion through the normal channels of democratic politics if we so desire, but the rights invoked by the Constitution do not insist upon it if society disagrees. From the perspective of either Textualism or Originalism, the text or intent of the Constitution leaves decisions of this nature in the hands of the peoples' representatives rather than the Court's Justices.

In a sense, the conclusion of *Roe* is very simple: the availability of abortion is protected by the Constitution. In another sense, it is much more complex, invoking a large number of constitutional controversies within one decision. It establishes new principles about privacy rights and new premises about the nature of a fetus. It is driven by clear positions on the role of judicial review, individual rights, federalism, ordered liberty, religion, and social facts. It offers a Living Constitutionalist conclusion with a Common Law implementation. *Roe* takes strong positions on six distinct points of conflict and intertwined aspects of two different schools of interpretation. If a reader disagrees with those positions, there is a lot to dislike. Combined with its clear moral implications, these divisions explain its enduring status as a lightning rod in American politics. This analysis of *Roe* helps us see not only why it is so controversial, but how the points of conflict and schools of interpretation shape important constitutional decisions.

17

CONTEMPORARY
LANDMARK CASES

From *Phelps* to Obamacare

Given all of this discussion of constitutional principles, premises, and precedents—of the nine points of conflict and how they relate to the four schools of thought—the real test is whether this system can help us understand constitutional controversies. As new constitutional questions come before the Justices, what does this understanding tell us about the rulings of the Court? Taking a recent year of the Court's decisions as a testing ground, three rulings stand out as contemporary landmarks: *Snyder v. Phelps* (2011), *Brown v. Plata* (2011), and *Wal-Mart v. Dukes* (2011). One of the most important recent decisions of the Court came the following year in *National Federation of Independent Business v. Sebelius* (2012), better known as the Affordable Care Act or Obamacare decision. This is such an important ruling—both to our national politics and for an understanding of the conflicts on the current Court—that it must be discussed. The analysis of *Roe* in the previous chapter illustrated how remarkably complex landmark decisions can be. But most cases are more simple and can be condensed to one or two points of conflict. *Phelps* is about whether the First Amendment's protections of free speech allow a civil court to award damages for hurtful speech; but in another sense the case is about the competing claims of ordered liberty versus pure liberty. *Plata* is about whether prison overcrowding that leads to a lack of medical attention is a violation of the Eighth Amendment's prohibition against cruel and unusual punishment; but underneath this, the case is about whether federal judges and Supreme Court Justices have an expansive power of judicial review. *Wal-Mart* is about whether a wage discrimination claim can seek a class action including all women employed by the corporation since 1998 (1.5 million claimants, creating the largest class action lawsuit to date in U.S. history); but at its heart the case is about the social fact of whether men and women must be assumed to be the same or whether it is possible that they may be systematically different. The Health Care Decision is about whether the sweeping changes to American medicine embodied in the Affordable Care Act are allowable uses of national power, including a federal mandate for individuals to purchase health insurance; but the ruling is essentially about federalism as a point of conflict and whether it is still a viable principle that limits the power of the national government, especially in regard to the meaning of the Interstate Commerce Clause. In an unexpected way, the decision also hinges on heavily disputed premise rulings about the nature of the congressional act and about the nature of health care in America. This final chapter briefly considers each of these cases in light of the nine points of conflict and four schools of interpretation.

Phelps

Judicial Review
Individual Versus Collective Rights
Federalism
Ordered Liberty
Religion
Transcendence
Premises
Precedent
Completeness

Living Constitutionalism	Common Law	Textualism	Originalism

We discussed the facts of the *Phelps* case earlier: a group that picketed a fallen Marine's funeral was held liable for damages by a civil jury, but the Court held that the First Amendment's guarantees of free speech disallowed the claim. *Phelps* takes a clear position on the primacy of individual rights over collective ones. In the realm of expression, our ability to regulate behavior (a collective right) must yield to a citizen's freedom to communicate (an individual right). The First

Amendment protection of free speech is fully individualized—it is not a collective right to information, but an individual freedom to act as one pleases.

The essence of the *Phelps* dispute is our constitutional understanding of liberty. A system of ordered liberty requires that rights be balanced by responsibilities. Therefore local government can restrict individual behavior in order to ensure a decent as well as free society. Pure liberty, on the other hand, insists upon no such limitations. Individual rights are not to be balanced, but to be upheld. Ordered liberty is the older standard, while pure liberty is the more recent. Regardless of which definition of liberty we prefer when given an individual choice, the question at hand is *Which does the Constitution require?*

Phelps represents an important shift in free speech law, because previous rulings had maintained a distinction between *political speech* that is fully protected by the First Amendment and mixed *speech-acts* that contain non-political speech or physical acts that have significant consequences. Under the old standard, an act of a non-political nature could be controlled by the community even if mixed with legitimate political expression. *Phelps* reverses this standard: an act is protected if it includes any political expression, regardless of its other aspects. The clearly political nature of the protest—aimed at public questions of war, gay marriage, etc.—overrides its clearly personal aspects aimed at the Snyder family.

It is easy to overlook that in this case we are not addressing the more dramatic invasions of free speech caused by government restrictions or criminal prosecutions. The state did not stop Phelps from protesting, nor charge the members of his group with a crime. He was held liable for the consequences of his speech, after a civil suit with a high burden of proof for showing damages. Nonetheless the Court ruled that the First Amendment shields citizens not only from government action but also from responsibility for any harm caused, applying the previous standards of criminal law to civil law as well. In rejecting the trial jury's ruling, the Court's decision suggests that ordered liberty is dead (at least as far as free speech is concerned), fully replaced by pure liberty as the constitutional definition of freedom.

The decision is clearly Living Constitutionalist, driven by the perceptions of pure liberty and individual rights. *Phelps* is about what the Constitution has come to mean, not what it explicitly says, or what its enduring principles mean as they were established at the Founding, or even what the Court has said the document means, but instead the newer, broader vision of unconstrained individual rights. This demands that pure liberty replace ordered liberty as our definition of constitutional freedoms in the realm of speech.

Plata

Judicial Review
Individual Versus Collective Rights
Federalism
Ordered Liberty
Religion
Transcendence
Premises
Precedent
Completeness

| **Living Constitutionalism** | Common Law | Textualism | Originalism |

The *Plata* case is about judicial review. It is a straightforward example of the dispute over the role of the judiciary in our system—whether federal judges and Supreme Court Justices are self-restrained actors who employ judicial review only to correct obvious errors by other branches of government or whether they are broadly empowered to interpret the Constitution and craft orders to enforce its concerns with social justice. In *Brown v. Plata* the Court split 5 to 4 on exactly this question.

The California prison system is overcrowded and has been the focus of many years of litigation regarding the resulting lack of adequate medical care for its prisoners. After several years of consideration, a panel of federal judges ordered the state to reduce the prison population to no more than 137.5% of its designed capacity, requiring the release of up to 46,000 prisoners. The unusual aspect of the order is that it is not a remedy for any specific violations of the Eighth Amendment but instead for a system-wide condition that makes individual violations more likely. The prisoners to be released are not the ones requiring medical care, but a group large enough so that the system can provide adequate care to the remaining population. In legal terms this is called a *structural injunction*, or an order to address a broad defect rather than the traditional method of addressing individual violations of rights. This is the focus of the dissent written by Justice Scalia, who argues that "if the court determines that a particular prisoner is being denied constitutionally required medical treatment, and the release of that prisoner (and no other remedy) would enable him to obtain medical treatment, then the court can order his release; but a court may not order the release of prisoners who have suffered no violations of their constitutional rights, merely to make it less likely that that will happen to them in the future." Scalia believes that the federal judges in this case made policy judgments properly allotted to the legislative branch (how to alter the prison system to make it work). Courts have veto power over existing policies, but not creative power over new ones, which is the responsibility of the legislature. This is what Scalia means in arguing that "structural injunctions, especially prisoner-release orders, raise grave separation-of-powers concerns and veer significantly from the historical role and institutional capacity of courts ... defying all sound conception of the proper role of judges."[82]

The specific issue on which the judges exerted their power is the scope of the constitutional protections of prisoners. Writing for the majority, Justice Kennedy argues that "prisoners retain the essence of human dignity inherent in all persons. Respect for that dignity animates the Eighth Amendment prohibition against cruel and unusual punishment ... Just as a prisoner may starve if not fed, he or she may suffer or die if not provided adequate medical care. A prison that deprives prisoners of basic sustenance, including adequate medical care, is incompatible with the concept of human dignity and has no place in civilized society."[83] Protecting this respect for human dignity requires a strong role for judges, who are able to issue structural injunctions that can address broad problems. The paradox of Kennedy's position is that felons who have violated the basic rules of society have the right to adequate health care, while honest citizens have no such right. Becoming a prisoner *creates* a right that does not exist prior to the offense. Many judges would argue that the heart of this perversity is that normal citizens *do not* have a right to health care rather than that felons *do*, but the perversity remains nonetheless.

Another aspect of the ruling is that individual rights to health care trump collective rights to social safety. While Scalia's dissent focuses on the conflict over the proper role of judicial review, Justice Alito concentrates on the potential social damage that the release order may cause, violating conceptions of collective rights:

> Before ordering any prisoner release, the PLRA (Prison Litigation Reform Act of 1995) commands a court to "give substantial weight to any adverse impact on public safety." ... in the early 1990s, federal courts enforced a cap on the number of inmates in the Philadelphia prison system, and thousands of inmates were set free. Although efforts were made to release only those prisoners who were least likely to commit violent crimes, that attempt was spectacularly unsuccessful. During an 18-month period, the Philadelphia police rearrested thousands of prisoners for committing 9,732 new crimes. Those defendants were charged with 79 murders, 90 rapes, 1,113 assaults, 959 robberies, 701 burglaries, and 2748 thefts.

For this reason, the Court's action is "a fundamental and dangerous error ... I fear that today's decision, like prior prisoner release orders, will lead to a grim roster of victims."[84]

The Court's decision is clearly from a Living Constitutionalist perspective, embracing a powerful judicial review, strong individual rights, and reading the Eighth Amendment as it has come to be understood by contemporary elites. The touchstone phrase of the Living Constitution—evolving standards of decency—originated in Eighth Amendment death penalty cases examining exactly this question of the definition of cruel and unusual punishment. In the Living Constitutionalist view, that definition is anything but static. The principle itself must evolve as society matures. If there is anywhere in our political system where the Constitution must be alive, it is how we treat criminal defendants and convicts because this is how the morality of a society is judged. This approach is in direct contrast to the ideals of ordered liberty, individual rights intertwined with social responsibilities, collective rights, and preservation, which distinguish the Originalist from the Living Constitutionalist positions. The 5 to 4 split among the Justices and the unusually strong dissents to the decision make the divisions clear. A case that appears to be about the prison system and the meaning of the Eighth Amendment is at heart about broader divisions over how we read the Constitution and the role of the judiciary.

Wal-Mart

Judicial Review
Individual Versus Collective Rights
Federalism
Ordered Liberty
Religion
Transcendence
Premises
Precedent
Completeness

Living Constitutionalism	Common Law	Textualism	**Originalism**

Unlike the previous two cases from this term, *Wal-Mart v. Dukes* is not about the power of judicial review or our understanding of rights and liberties. No specific constitutional principle is at issue. Instead it is a question of social fact. But like many rulings on premises, the decision does not address the topic directly nor admit that it is the central question at hand. The Court also does not identify the standard it employs for knowing which premise is accurate. There is no discussion of whether the Court will wait for society to endorse a new premise or whether it should move ahead of the current social norm. But the case revolves around a single question: *Are women and men the same?* Must our legal decisions assume that the two are equivalent or can they allow for the possibility of systematic differences between them?

The premise about men and women is the heart of the case because of the unusual legal claim made by the plaintiffs, a group who wish to bring a class action suit representing *all* female employees of Wal-Mart, present and past (since 1998). This includes approximately 1.5 million potential plaintiffs, which would create the largest class action suit in U.S. history. Class action suits break the normal pattern in our legal system of specific trials for specific injuries to specific plaintiffs, but they can be carried forward if they meet certain requirements. The heart of the legal question in *Wal-Mart* is whether all of the female employees do in fact create a class for the purposes of a discrimination lawsuit. The nine Justices agreed that the question of whether a group can be certified as a class is governed by Federal Rule of Civil Procedure 23. Among other requirements, Rule 23 cannot be met unless "there are questions of law or fact common to the class." In the majority opinion, Justice Scalia writes, "in this case, proof of commonality necessarily overlaps with respondents' merits contention that Wal-Mart engages in a *pattern or practice* of discrimination" (italics in original).[85] This does not sound like the key sentence of a decision, but it is. Class status requires a common situation of its members rather than the individual variation that would indicate separate proceedings. The plaintiffs are making the unusually broad claim that *all* women who have worked for Wal-Mart are in the same class. Whether or not this is true depends on evidence of commonality or the similar treatment of all of the plaintiffs throughout the thousands of Wal-Mart stores, which the majority does not believe because the evidence for it relies on the premise that men and women are the same.

The plaintiffs' evidence is statistical. Wal-Mart has a policy of allowing individual managers in its stores to make salary and promotion decisions based on their judgment of the workers. Each manager's incentive is to pick the best people so the store runs smoothly and makes as much money as possible; he decides which employees are offered promotions to management and which get paid more than others in the same position (within a $2 an hour range). Women comprise approximately 70% of the hourly employees, but only 30% of the selections to management. Likewise, women in each job category were given lower pay raises on average than men in the same category. Wal-Mart's executives had no centralized control over these decisions, but the aggregate effect of individual managers making thousands of judgments created a disparity of outcomes between male and female employees. The crux of the legal claim is that if the decisions had been fairly applied, then the pay and promotion decisions would not have this sort of disparate outcome; discrimination on the basis of sex is the only possible cause of this and therefore *all* women were affected. This creates a class in the traditional sense, allowing the plaintiffs to sue for the back pay that would have gone to each female employee if they had been paid and promoted at the same rate as men. The logic of the claim is clear: men and women are the same and therefore would be chosen equally in any neutral system. They clearly were *not* chosen equally; therefore the system must discriminate against women.

This logic is indisputable if each part of the argument is accurate. But is discrimination the only possible cause of the disparity in promotion and pay? Is it *possible* that men and women are different or do we simply have to throw that out as a logical impossibility? Is it possible the men worked harder? Is it possible they were more efficient at the job? Is it possible they were better managers of other employees? Is it possible they were more eager for promotion? Or is it possible, as many sociologists argue, that men on average have lower family and household duties that allow them to focus more on work? Are any of these or any other factor *possible*? If they are, then simple aggregate evidence that men are promoted more than women is not evidence of discrimination. Each individual plaintiff would have to show evidence of discrimination in her specific case. But if these things are simply *impossible*—if it is ruled out as a logical impossibility that there are actual performance differences between women and men—then the statistical evidence indicates discrimination and the class action should be allowed to continue. The crux of the issue is this: is it possible that men and women display differences in job performance or is this simply an impossibility?

The majority concludes that the plaintiffs

> have identified no "specific employment practice"—much less one that ties all 1.5 million claims together. Merely showing that Wal-Mart's policy of discretion has produced an overall sex-based disparity does not suffice... Some managers will claim that the availability of women, or qualified women, or interested women, in their stores' area does not mirror the national or regional statistics. And almost all of them will claim to have been applying some sex-neutral, performance-based criteria—whose nature and effects will differ from store to store.[86]

Scalia does not phrase it directly, but what this means is that it is in fact possible that the male and female employees were simply different and therefore that different outcomes were not due to discrimination.

The four dissenters saw it differently. Justice Ginsburg writes that

> the plaintiffs' evidence, including class members' tales of their own experiences, suggests that gender bias suffused Wal-Mart's company culture. ... the plaintiffs presented an expert's appraisal to show that the pay and promotions disparities at Wal-Mart "can be explained only by gender discrimination and not by ... neutral variables." ... The results, the District Court found, were sufficient to raise an "inference of discrimination."[87]

In other words, Ginsburg (like the plaintiffs) finds it highly unlikely, if not impossible, that disparities in the aggregate numbers of promotions to men and women could be accounted for by legitimate differences between the two groups. In her view the appropriate premise of the law is that men and women are the same, as opposed to the majority's premise that it is possible that the two groups are systematically different.

The Health Care Decision

Judicial Review
Individual Versus Collective Rights
Federalism
Ordered Liberty
Religion
Transcendence
Premises
Precedent
Completeness

Living Constitutionalism	**Common Law**	Textualism	**Originalism**

The case is *National Federation of Independent Business et al v. Sebelius* but it is unlikely to be known as anything but the Obamacare

Decision, perhaps more politely as the Affordable Care Act (ACA) Decision. In 2010 the Congress passed and President Obama signed a sweeping reform aiming to dramatically increase the number of Americans who have access to health care. Its two central mechanisms are a mandate that all citizens who can afford to do so buy a health insurance policy (subsidized by the federal government depending on personal income) and an expansion of the Medicaid system to cover citizens whose incomes do not allow them to buy their own insurance (up to 133% of the poverty line). Each congressional action challenges the principle of federalism—the first through Congress' broad interpretation of its powers under the Interstate Commerce Clause and the second by Congress' attempt to implement its own policies through the institutions of state governments. The question in both cases is whether the national government exceeded its bounds. In the first case it may be outside of the limits of the Commerce Clause to require individual citizens to make a specific purchase, compelling entry into a market rather than regulating existing economic activity that influences interstate commerce. And in the second case it may violate the principle of federalism if the national government compels state governments to take action within their own realm of sovereignty and spend their own money doing it. On both questions of principle the Health Care Decision provides clear answers, but it also offers a crucial premise ruling that alters the outcome in an unexpected way. The decision illustrates clearly the interwoven nature of principles and premises in constitutional controversies.

The introduction to the decision, written by Chief Justice John Roberts, is devoted to a statement of broad constitutional foundations, concluding that "the questions before us must be considered against the backdrop of these basic principles." The most critical of these is federalism. The second paragraph begins, "In our federal system, the National Government possesses only limited powers; the States and the people retain the remainder." Roberts continues with a strong rendition of structural limits to the national government: "Today, the restrictions on government power foremost in many Americans' minds are likely to be affirmative prohibitions, such as contained in the Bill of Rights. These affirmative prohibitions come into play, however, only where the Government possesses authority to act in the first place ... The Federal Government has expanded dramatically in over the past two centuries, but it still must show that a constitutional grant of power authorizes each of its actions."[88] The point of conflict at issue here is clearly federalism, both in its broad principle of dual sovereignty between the national and state governments (potentially violated by the Medicaid expansion), and in the specific meaning of the Interstate Commerce Clause (potentially violated by the individual mandate). The Commerce Clause is either a meaningful limit to federal power designed to retain lasting force, or it is a practical statement designed to create government options as well as restrictions, especially in response to the challenges brought by the growth of the national economy.

The decision takes a clear stand on the Federalist side of this dispute, ruling that the individual mandate is outside of the bounds of Congress' power under the Commerce Clause. If that power includes the ability to compel economic activity, then it is difficult to identify a discernible limit to congressional authority. Roberts draws a clear distinction between economic activity and *inactivity*: "Congress has never attempted to rely on that power to compel individuals not engaged in commerce to purchase an unwanted product." This is the case because "the power to *regulate* commerce presupposes the existence of commercial activity to be regulated. If the power to 'regulate' something included the power to create it, many of the provisions in the Constitution would be superfluous ... Construing the Commerce Clause to permit Congress to regulate individuals precisely *because* they are doing nothing would open a new and potentially vast domain to congressional authority."[89] Roberts concludes that "Congress already enjoys vast power to regulate much of what we do. Accepting the Government's theory would give Congress the same license to regulate what we do not do, fundamentally changing the relation between the citizen and the Federal government."[90]

The ruling takes a similar stand on the Medicaid expansion. The changes envisioned by the ACA are achieved by requiring state governments to administer the program and pay for a part of its costs out of their own budgets; refusal to do so would result in losing their existing federal funding for current Medicaid payments. In its previous form, Medicaid focused on providing health care for citizens with severe needs such as the disabled, blind, and children living in poverty. Under the ACA, it expands to serve the entire adult population below one and a third of the poverty line, partially funded by the federal budget and partly by states' own resources. There is nothing new about federal grants coming with conditions in order to receive the funds, but the Court has maintained that these agreements are in the nature of a contract, which must be voluntarily accepted by the states rather than compelled. In this case, Roberts characterizes Congress' offer as "a gun to the head." Many states would lose over 10 percent of their entire budgets if the existing Medicaid funding were cut off, amounting to "economic dragooning that leaves the States with no real option but to acquiesce in the Medicaid expansion." Therefore Roberts concludes that the Constitution forbids this sort of compulsion of state governments: "As a practical matter, that means States may now choose to reject the expansion."[91] Not only the Chief Justice and the other conservatives agreed with this position, but also Justices Breyer and Kagan, giving this part of the ruling the strongest majority of 7/2.

Perhaps the clearest way to illustrate the division over federalism is not from the controlling decision but from the competing dissents. According to Justice Scalia (joined by Alito, Kennedy, and Thomas):

> What is absolutely clear, affirmed by the text of the 1789 Constitution, by the Tenth Amendment ratified in 1791, and by innumerable cases of ours in the 220 years since, is that there are structural limits upon federal power ... [These limits cannot] enable the Federal Government to regulate all private conduct and to compel the States to function as administrators of federal programs.[92]

But according to Justice Ginsburg (joined by Breyer, Kagan, and Sotomayor):

> This rigid reading of the [Commerce] Clause makes scant sense and is stunningly retrogressive. Since 1937, our precedent has recognized Congress' large authority to set the Nation's course in the economic and social welfare realm ... This capacious power extends even to local activities that, viewed in the aggregate, have a substantial impact on interstate commerce ... Far from trampling on States' sovereignty, the ACA attempts a federal solution for the very reason that the States, acting separately, cannot meet the need ... Why should the Chief Justice strive so mightily to hem in Con-

gress' capacity to meet the new problems arising constantly in our ever-developing modern economy?[93]

In other words, either federalism is real and permanent, there are structural as well as rights-based limits to national power that still apply, and therefore the Commerce Clause is not a blank check for congressional action, or the United States is now a national entity that makes federalism anachronistic, our massive economic growth has expanded the power of the federal government through the Interstate Commerce as well as Necessary and Proper Clauses, and we must give deference to federal problem-solving efforts when "Congress was able to achieve a practical, altogether reasonable, solution."[94]

Which side has the better of it depends on our evaluation of the point of conflict over federalism. It may be alive or dead, or in a weakened state somewhere in between. Either the Fourteenth Amendment has wrought deep changes in the structure and meaning of the Constitution, or the original principles remain in force. The Interstate Commerce Clause is either an expanding grant of power to the national government as circumstances warrant, or it is a structural limit to national power crucial to the maintenance of individual and collective liberty. The slimmest majority of five Justices agree that federalism is still a cornerstone of our system and the limits to national power are to be observed.

However—and there is a tremendous however—the ruling does not stop here. As Roberts phrases it, "That is not the end of the matter." The decision concludes that even though the Commerce Clause is not sufficient, the Court must examine every available avenue of congressional power. One of these is the power to levy taxes. The individual mandate is enforced by an additional payment when filing federal income taxes if a citizen cannot show that they have purchased health insurance. Therefore "the government asks us to read the mandate not as ordering individuals to buy insurance, but rather as imposing a tax on those who do not buy that product."[95] To quote the critical parts of Roberts' thinking: "It is well established that if a statute has two possible meanings, one of which violates the Constitution, courts should adopt the meaning that does not do so ... The question is not whether that is the most natural interpretation of the mandate, but only whether it is a 'fairly possible' one ... The most straightforward reading of the mandate is that it commands individuals to purchase insurance"; however, "the mandate can be regarded as establishing a condition—not owning health insurance—that triggers a tax—the required payment to the IRS." This means that "The Federal Government does not have the power to order people to buy health insurance. Section 5000A [the mandate] would therefore be unconstitutional if read as a command. The Federal Government does have the power to impose a tax on those without health insurance. Section 5000A is therefore constitutional, because it can reasonably be read as a tax."[96]

This part of the decision is difficult to understand on a first reading, mostly because an earlier section of the ruling clearly states that the individual mandate is *not* a tax. The Court considered a challenge to the entire lawsuit grounded in the Anti-Injunction Act; this is an old law that citizens cannot challenge the constitutionality of a new tax until it has been paid. The ACA penalties do not go into effect until 2014, which would delay the possibility of a federal suit until that time if the payments are in fact a tax. The Court rules that they are not, which allows the health care case to be heard and decided. So the mandate both *is* and *is not* a tax, depending on the question at hand.

Roberts' reasoning is that the mandate is not a tax because Congress says it is not in the text of the law, and since Congress also wrote the Anti-Injunction Act, Congress is best situated to decide how its two actions relate to each other. By calling it a penalty, clearly Congress meant for the Anti-Injunction Act to not apply. However, when deciding the *constitutionality* of the new act as opposed to how an existing statute applies to it, the Supreme Court must decide what it really is (or what it can be construed to be at its broadest interpretation) and in that sense it *is* a tax. To be clear, Roberts is not saying that the mandate is categorically either a tax or not; instead he is saying that *if it can be considered a tax in some sense, it can be constitutional.* Roberts is offering an unusual premise theory: *any premise that saves constitutionality should be employed.* Regardless of "magic words or labels," or even the language of the act itself ("It is of course true that the Act describes the payment as a 'penalty' and not a 'tax'"), the role of the Court is to apply the broadest possible interpretation to a legislative act in order to arrive at a constitutional conclusion.[97] This is a departure from Roberts' usual means of interpretation, which is closest to Originalism. In the ACA decision he accepts a Common Law approach that allows for malleable and emerging premises, geared toward crafting new workable solutions to national problems. This is especially striking because the single premise ruling overrides the expected conclusion from his stand on principles, in the end allowing the individual mandate to be constitutional. The ruling represents a rare occurrence in Roberts' thinking of Originalist principles paired with Common Law premises, setting him apart in this decision from the other Originalist Justices.

The conservative dissenters believe that this kind of dual definition defeats the idea of clear constitutional government that can be understood by normal citizens. By invoking this specific method of determining a premise, the decision creates "a creature never hitherto seen in the United States Reports: A penalty for constitutional purposes that is *also* a tax for constitutional purposes. In all our cases the two are mutually exclusive. The provision challenged under the Constitution is either a penalty or else a tax." In his characteristic attacking fashion, Scalia writes that "we have never held—*never*—that a penalty imposed for violation of the law was so trivial as to be in effect a tax. We have never held that *any* exaction imposed for violation of the law is an exercise of Congress' tax power—even when the statute *calls* it a tax, much less when (as here) the statute repeatedly calls it a penalty." Therefore "to say that the Individual Mandate merely imposes a tax is not to interpret the statute but to rewrite it ... confusing the question of what Congress *did* with the question of what Congress *could have done*," which "carries verbal wizardry too far, deep into the forbidden land of the sophists."[98]

Scalia's objection to renaming a regulatory penalty a tax is not only that it is confusing wordplay, but that it commits electoral as well as constitutional fraud: the constitutional requirement that tax measures originate in the House of Representatives is designed to make taxing and spending decisions directly accountable to the voters. If the Congress can tell voters a new measure is not a tax, but then the Court will later identify it as a tax in order to maintain its constitutionality, then our elected officials can dodge responsibility for their actions. The Justices of the Court cannot be voted out of office and hence can be enlisted unwillingly into doing the dirty work of the Members of Congress.

The premise that the individual mandate is a tax for constitutional purposes was accepted by five of the Justices but rejected by the other four. However, another premise is also at issue, which failed to carry the day by only receiving the support of four dissenters. Ginsburg strongly holds that *everyone in America is active in the health care market whether they wish to be or not.*[99] There is no such thing as a citizen who is not going to need health care at some point in the future. Everyone might need (or want) a car, but they have to pay for it out of their own pocket. Health care, however, is not something we deny to our fellow citizens: "Unlike the markets for most products ... the inability to pay for care does not mean that an uninsured individual will receive no care. Federal and state law, as well as professional obligations and embedded social norms, require hospitals and physicians to provide care when it is most needed, regardless of the patient's ability to pay."[100] Health care is now viewed by many Americans as more of a right than an economic product to be purchased.

Not only is health care a product that everyone consumes and no one can be denied, but the way we pay for it is also unique. Because it is a partially communitarian good, those with health insurance pay significantly higher rates to cover the costs of the uninsured care given in emergency rooms and hospitals. Ginsburg's bottom line is that "those with health insurance subsidize the medical care of those without it"; therefore "every uninsured person impacts the market price of medical care and medical insurance."[101] Not only are all Americans in the health *care* market, but they are in the health *insurance* market as well, simply because the two things have become the same in contemporary America. Health insurance is no longer just a hedge against future risk, but is the normal payment mechanism for usual and expected health costs. Ginsburg can therefore conclude that "health insurance is a means of paying for this care, nothing more. In requiring individuals to obtain insurance, Congress is therefore not mandating the purchase of a discrete, unwanted product. Rather, Congress is merely defining the terms on which individuals pay for an interstate good they consume."[102] Given these perceptions about health care, the four liberal dissenters advocate a more communitarian premise that may be highly influential if it gains strength in the future.

In his competing dissent, Scalia disputes Ginsburg's perception of social reality, asserting that young people who are not interested in purchasing health insurance "are quite simply not participants in that market, and cannot be made so (and thereby subjected to regulation) by the simple device of defining participants to include all those who will, later in their lifetime, probably purchase the goods or services covered by the mandated insurance. Such a definition of market participants is unprecedented, and were it to be a premise for the exercise of national power, it would have no principled limits." Scalia concludes "it is true that, at the end of the day, it is inevitable that each American will affect commerce and become a part of it, even if not by choice. But if every person comes within the Commerce Clause power of Congress to regulate by the simple reason that he will one day engage in commerce, the idea of limited Government power is at an end."[103] This is perhaps our clearest example of the interwoven nature of premises and principles, with one or the other social fact about the nature of health care contributing to very different conclusions about the principles of the Constitution.

Given all of these considerations, Roberts provides a clear summary of the ruling:

> The Affordable Care Act is constitutional in part and unconstitutional in part. The individual mandate cannot be upheld as an exercise of Congress' power under the Commerce Clause. That Clause authorizes Congress to regulate interstate commerce, not to order individuals to engage in it. In this case, however, it is reasonable to construe what Congress has done as increasing taxes on those who have a certain amount of income, but choose to go without health insurance. Such legislation is within Congress's power to tax.
>
> As far as the Medicaid expansion, that portion of the Affordable Care Act violates the Constitution by threatening existing Medicaid funding. Congress has no authority to order the States to regulate according to its instructions. Congress may offer the States grants and require the States to comply with accompanying conditions, but the States must have a genuine choice whether to accept the offer.[104]

Unlike many of the previous rulings we have discussed, the Health Care Decision only appears to be a 5/4 split on the Court. The ruling is not truly 5/4, but 4/1/4. There is only one Justice in the majority—Roberts himself—while there are four who agree with one part of his ruling and dissent to another part, with the other four dissenters

Table 17.1 Principle and Premise in the Health Care Decision

Principle	Premise	4 Liberal Dissenters	1 Chief Justice	4 Conservative Dissenters
Federalism		No	Yes	Yes
	Mandate*	Yes	Yes	No
	Health Care**	Yes	No	No

* The individual mandate can be considered a tax for constitutional purposes, when giving it the broadest possible construction.

** Health care is distinct from other products because (1) everyone is in the market continuously, and (2) the health insurance market is operationally the same thing as the health care market.

taking the reverse positions. The four conservatives in dissent argue that his ruling is correct on federalism while the premise ruling is faulty; the four liberal dissenters dispute the role of federalism while accepting the premise that allows the mandate to be considered a tax. Roberts is alone in his combined position. Table 17.1 above illustrates the divisions among the Chief Justice and the competing dissenters on the principle and premises at issue.

In an unusual fashion, the Health Care Decision combines Originalist principles in support of federalism with a Common Law approach to premises. This is rarely seen, was not predicted, and explains the 4/1/4 structure of the decision and the dissents. The controversy and its outcome are difficult to follow without first seeing the longstanding dispute over federalism as a constitutional principle, grounded in the competing readings of the document that make the concept either crucial or anachronistic. The second key to the decision is the central role of premise rulings and their justifications in constitutional controversies. Considered together, these two elements explain a complex and influential ruling.

The four recent landmark decisions address both principle and premise. They uphold pure liberty over ordered liberty, and individual rights over collective ones. They endorse an expansive judicial review rather than a restrained approach to judicial power. They are often oriented to a Living Constitutionalist approach, grounded in positive views of judicial review, pure liberty, and individual rights, allowing the Constitution to be read in a broad and evolving way. But the Court was not exclusively controlled by the Living Constitutionalists.

The premise decision in *Wal-Mart* was guided by the Originalist view that the Court should recognize only the current social premises rather than moving ahead to a newer premise that is not fully accepted by our society. The healthcare decision was a mixed bag: the ruling on principle—that federalism and the Commerce Clause create real limits to national power—is Originalist, striking down the Medicaid expansion and potentially the individual mandate, while the ruling on premise was made with a more expansive Common Law standard granting deference to new solutions to national problems, allowing the mandate to proceed. The healthcare ruling is a nuanced decision that highlights the role of both principle and premise in constitutional controversies. It is worth noting that three of the four recent landmark cases were decided by the slimmest majority of five Justices, inspiring strong dissents. The Court maintains an interesting balance among its schools of thought and its allegiances to the competing sides of the points of conflict. With these divisions in mind we can understand what its rulings truly mean.

CONCLUSION

Reading the Constitution for Ourselves

The Constitution belongs to the American people, but is interpreted by the Justices of the Supreme Court. How they read our founding document is guided by several underlying conflicts that shape their views and influence their decisions. In order to arrive at our own perception of the Constitution, we must understand these enduring conflicts—how the Justices of the Court see them and how we see them. We have identified *nine points of conflict*, which add up to *four distinct schools of interpretation*. The debates over the legitimacy of judicial review, the nature of rights, federalism, ordered liberty, religion, transcendence, social facts, precedent, and completeness all add up to the competing schools of Textualism, Common Law Constitutionalism, Originalism, and Living Constitutionalism. How these distinct approaches see the principles, premises, and precedents of the Constitution leads them to very different conclusions about how it should be understood. The purpose of this book is to sort out which way of reading the Constitution makes the most sense to you. There are several conflicts to consider, but they lead to a clearer understanding of our system.

It is easy to assume that what the Supreme Court says is what the Constitution means. We rely on the Justices to speak for the nation, but we also have the right and duty to read the Constitution for ourselves. Textualists make a strong point that our Constitution is meant to be read and understood by us. Even if we are more persuaded by one of the other schools of thought that require additional reading beyond the text alone, we can still come to grips with what the document and our traditions mean. A Common Law approach requires more knowledge of the precedents and history of the Court; Originalism demands a greater understanding of the Founding era; and Living Constitutionalism relies on a perception of evolving contemporary beliefs. With each of these approaches to the Constitution we have the opportunity to understand for ourselves what our core document means.

GLOSSARY OF TERMS

Article I   the first Article of the Constitution, dealing with the
Legislative Branch (election, rules, powers, and limitations of
Congress)

Article II   the Executive Branch (election and powers of the
president)

Article III   the Judicial Branch (selection, powers, and limits of the
Supreme Court)

Article IV   interstate relations (full faith and credit among states;
extradition; new states; guarantee of republican government)

Article V   amendment

Article VI   the Nation as a whole (debts; Supremacy Clause; oaths
of office)

Article VII   ratification

balancing   a convention of reading the Constitution; because
the Constitution embodies contradictions, some parts must be
weighed or balanced against others

Bill of Rights   the first ten amendments to the Constitution, proposed by the 1st Congress in 1789 and enacted in 1791 after ratification by the states, designed (as stated in the preamble written
by the 1st Congress) "to prevent misconstruction or abuse of its
powers" by adding "further declaratory and restrictive clauses"

bong hits   what one does for Jesus (in Alaska), see *Morse v. Frederick*
(2007)

chronological reading   a convention of reading the Constitution;
because of the amendment process, parts of the document are
altered by later parts, especially the Fourteenth Amendment

Common Law Constitutionalism   one of the four major schools of constitutional interpretation, grounded in the idea that respect for precedent creates the best foundation for a stable system, and new circumstances should be dealt with through incremental changes that offer workable rules

compelling state interest   the standard to override a fundamental right under the strict scrutiny test, that the government is pursuing a necessary goal, which cannot be achieved by less restrictive means

comprehensive reading   a disputed convention of reading the Constitution, that we should not read clause by clause, but take the whole document into consideration, which leads to the concept of transcendence

concurring opinion   agrees with the outcome of who won the case, but disputes the reasoning on which it should be based

differentiation   a convention of reading the Constitution, that each word has a distinct meaning and does not repeat other parts of the document

due process   a constitutional principle that recognized legal procedures must be followed, ruling out arbitrary government action; grounded in the Fifth and Fourteenth Amendments

equal protection   a constitutional principle that all persons must be accorded the same rights, regardless of category distinctions such as race, gender, or religion

evolving standards of decency   a foundation of a living constitutional approach, the idea that as we grow as a society our principles evolve with us, such that something that did not violate the Constitution earlier may do so now

federalism   the constitutional principle that our system divides powers between the national and local governments, maintaining a large realm of local autonomy

fighting words   a Supreme Court precedent that expressions which by their very nature are likely to inspire a violent response are not protected by the First Amendment (*Chaplinsky v. New Hampshire*, 1942)

fundamental right   a right that is "intrinsic to a scheme of ordered liberty," i.e., the constitutional order of individual liberty and dignity would be significantly harmed if the right were violated

fundamental rights doctrine the Supreme Court doctrine that some rights are fundamental and some are not; those that are fundamental are incorporated against state governments and receive the highest form of constitutional protection, requiring strict scrutiny (see *incorporation, selective incorporation, total incorporation*)

incorporation the effect of the Fourteenth Amendment applying the Bill of Rights to state and local government as well as federal actions (see *selective incorporation* and *total incorporation*)

Interstate Commerce Clause the constitutional provision in Article I allowing the Legislative Branch to regulate certain kinds of economic transactions, it has been a foundation of the expansion of federal power; from a Federalist perspective the clause applies only to transactions that are truly national in scope, while local trade is outside of federal bounds; from a Living Constitutionalist perspective the clause has broadened federal power as interstate trade has affected more aspects of American life and the realm of truly local trade has decreased

Living Constitutionalism one of the four major schools of constitutional interpretation, grounded in the idea that as society evolves, the principles as well as premises of the Constitution adapt to the needs of the people

Morse *Morse v. Frederick* (2007), a school speech case that upheld the ability of public schools to control speech that invoked drug references, known as the Bong Hits for Jesus Case

ordered liberty the constitutional principle that rights and responsibilities are linked, specifically that the individual liberty to act is combined with the collective liberty to maintain a decent society; the balance between individual freedom and local regulatory power

Originalism one of the four major schools of constitutional interpretation, grounded in the idea that the intent or meaning of the document established by the Founders is the guiding means of understanding the Constitution

Phelps *Snyder v. Phelps* (2011), a major free speech case on the limits of indecent behavior in a free society; disallowed the ability of individual citizens to hold others accountable for intentional emotional distress in a civil action if the speech in question has a political component

police power   the ability of local government to regulate society for the protection of the safety, health, and morals of citizens

preamble   the fifty-two words introducing the Constitution, discussing the actors, actions, and purposes of the document

precedent   a prior decision of the Supreme Court, which the Court should respect under the principle of *stare decisis*

premise (aka social fact)   a reality constructed by collective belief, such as the personhood or non-personhood of fetuses

privacy   a protected constitutional liberty under the line of cases beginning with *Griswold*, that intimate personal decisions are outside of the realm of government control

Privileges and Immunities Clause   one of the three key clauses of the Fourteenth Amendment, providing all constitutional protections against state and local government, although this line of protection was ignored following the Slaughter House Cases in favor of selective incorporation of the Bill of Rights against the states

pure liberty   the newer interpretation of freedom, opposed to ordered liberty, the idea that individuals are free to act unless they cause direct harm to others (see J. S. Mill "On Liberty")

rational basis   the lower standard for considering the constitutionality of government actions, applied by the Supreme Court to protections that are not fundamental

Roe   *Roe v. Wade* (1973), the Supreme Court case that established the constitutional protect of legal abortion, grounded in a fundamental right of privacy

selective incorporation   the position that the Fourteenth Amendment did not fully apply constitutional protections against local government, but only those that can be identified as fundamental

social fact (aka premise)   a reality constructed by collective belief, such as the personhood or nonpersonhood of fetuses

stare decisis   Latin for "that which has been decided," the principle of following previous decisions or precedents

strict scrutiny   the prevailing standard for abridging a fundamental right, requiring a compelling state interest

substantive due process   the concrete requirements of liberty and justice protected by the due process clauses of the Fifth and Fourteenth Amendments

Textualism   one of the four major schools of constitutional interpretation, grounded in the idea that the language of the document is all that is necessary to understand its meaning

Tinker   *Tinker v. DesMoines* (1969), a major school speech case, ruling that student expression that is disruptive of the educational mission of the school can be controlled but non-disruptive speech cannot

total incorporation   the position that the Privileges and Immunities Clause of the Fourteenth Amendment immediately applied all constitutional protections against state and local government

transcendence   the idea that the Constitution is more than the sum of its parts, such that when read as a whole it embodies broader principles than the specific enumerated rights; the whole is more than the sum of its parts; liberty is the most frequently invoked transcendent principle, while possible others are equality or preservation

THE CONSTITUTION

We the people of the United States, in order to form
a **more perfect union**, establish **justice**, insure **domestic
tranquility**, provide for the **common defense**, promote the
general welfare, and secure the blessings of **liberty** to ourselves
and our posterity, do **ordain and establish** this Constitution
for the United States of America.

Article I (*Legislative Branch*)

Section 1. All legislative powers herein granted shall be vested in a
Congress of the United States, which shall consist of a Senate and
House of Representatives.

Section 2. The **House of Representatives** shall be composed of members chosen every second year by the people of the several states, and
the electors in each state shall have the qualifications requisite for electors of the most numerous branch of the state legislature.

No person shall be a Representative who shall not have attained to the
age of **twenty five years**, and been seven years a citizen of the United
States, and who shall not, when elected, be an inhabitant of that state
in which he shall be chosen.

Representatives and direct taxes shall be apportioned among the several states which may be included within this union, according to their
respective numbers, which shall be determined by adding to the whole

number of free persons, including those bound to service for a term of years, and excluding Indians not taxed, three fifths of all other Persons. The actual Enumeration shall be made within three years after the first meeting of the Congress of the United States, and within every subsequent term of ten years, in such manner as they shall by law direct. The number of Representatives shall not exceed one for every thirty thousand, but each state shall have at least one Representative; and until such enumeration shall be made, the state of New Hampshire shall be entitled to chuse three, Massachusetts eight, Rhode Island and Providence Plantations one, Connecticut five, New York six, New Jersey four, Pennsylvania eight, Delaware one, Maryland six, Virginia ten, North Carolina five, South Carolina five, and Georgia three.

When vacancies happen in the Representation from any state, the executive authority thereof shall issue writs of election to fill such vacancies.

The House of Representatives shall choose their speaker and other officers; and shall have the sole power of impeachment.

Section 3. The **Senate** of the United States shall be composed of **two Senators from each state**, chosen by the legislature thereof, for six years; and each Senator shall have one vote. (*superseded by 17th Amendment*)

Immediately after they shall be assembled in consequence of the first election, they shall be divided as equally as may be into three classes. The seats of the Senators of the first class shall be vacated at the expiration of the second year, of the second class at the expiration of the fourth year, and the third class at the expiration of the sixth year, so that one third may be chosen every second year; and if vacancies happen by resignation, or otherwise, during the recess of the legislature of any state, the executive thereof may make temporary appointments until the next meeting of the legislature, which shall then fill such vacancies.

No person shall be a Senator who shall not have attained to the age of **thirty years**, and been nine years a citizen of the United States and who shall not, when elected, be an inhabitant of that state for which he shall be chosen.

The Vice President of the United States shall be President of the Senate, but shall have no vote, unless they be equally divided.

The Senate shall choose their other officers, and also a President pro tempore, in the absence of the Vice President, or when he shall exercise the office of President of the United States.

The Senate shall have the sole power to try all impeachments. When sitting for that purpose, they shall be on oath or affirmation. When the President of the United States is tried, the Chief Justice shall preside: And no person shall be convicted without the concurrence of two thirds of the members present.

Judgment in cases of impeachment shall not extend further than to removal from office, and disqualification to hold and enjoy any office of honor, trust or profit under the United States: but the party convicted shall nevertheless be liable and subject to indictment, trial, judgment and punishment, according to law.

Section 4. The times, places and manner of holding elections for Senators and Representatives, shall be prescribed in each state by the legislature thereof; but the Congress may at any time by law make or alter such regulations, except as to the places of choosing Senators. The Congress shall assemble at least once in every year, and such meeting shall be on the first Monday in December, unless they shall by law appoint a different day.

Section 5. Each House shall be the judge of the elections, returns and qualifications of its own members, and a majority of each shall constitute a quorum to do business; but a smaller number may adjourn from day to day, and may be authorized to compel the attendance of absent members, in such manner, and under such penalties as each House may provide.

Each House may determine the rules of its proceedings, punish its members for disorderly behavior, and, with the concurrence of two thirds, expel a member.

Each House shall keep a journal of its proceedings, and from time to time publish the same, excepting such parts as may in their judgment require secrecy; and the yeas and nays of the members of either House on any question shall, at the desire of one fifth of those present, be entered on the journal.

Neither House, during the session of Congress, shall, without the consent of the other, adjourn for more than three days, nor to any other place than that in which the two Houses shall be sitting.

Section 6. The Senators and Representatives shall receive a compensation for their services, to be ascertained by law, and paid out of the treasury of the United States. They shall in all cases, except treason, felony and breach of the peace, be privileged from arrest during their attendance at the session of their respective Houses, and in going to and returning from the same; and for any speech or debate in either House, they shall not be questioned in any other place.

No Senator or Representative shall, during the time for which he was elected, be appointed to any civil office under the authority of the United States, which shall have been created, or the emoluments whereof shall have been increased during such time: and no person holding any office under the United States, shall be a member of either House during his continuance in office.

Section 7. All bills for raising revenue shall originate in the House of Representatives; but the Senate may propose or concur with amendments as on other Bills.

Every bill which shall have passed the House of Representatives and the Senate, **shall, before it become a law, be presented to the President of the United States**; if he approve he shall sign it, but if not he shall return it, with his objections to that House in which it shall have originated, who shall enter the objections at large on their journal, and proceed to reconsider it. **If after such reconsideration two thirds of that House shall agree to pass the bill**, it shall be sent, together with the objections, to the other House, by which it shall likewise be reconsidered, and **if approved by two thirds of that House, it shall become a law**. But in all such cases the votes of both Houses shall be determined by yeas and nays, and the names of the persons voting for and against the bill shall be entered on the journal of each House respectively. If any bill shall not be returned by the President within ten days (Sundays excepted) after it shall have been presented to him, the same shall be a law, in like manner as if he had signed it, unless the Congress by their adjournment prevent its return, in which case it shall not be a law.

Every order, resolution, or vote to which the concurrence of the Senate and House of Representatives may be necessary (except on a question of adjournment) shall be presented to the President of the United States; and before the same shall take effect, shall be approved by him, or being disapproved by him, shall be repassed by two thirds of the Senate and House of Representatives, according to the rules and limitations prescribed in the case of a bill.

Section 8. The Congress shall have **power to lay and collect taxes**, duties, imposts and excises, to pay the debts and provide for the common defense and general welfare of the United States; but all duties, imposts and excises shall be uniform throughout the United States;

To borrow money on the credit of the United States;

To regulate commerce with foreign nations, and **among the several states**, and with the Indian tribes; (*Interstate Commerce Clause*)

To establish a uniform rule of naturalization, and uniform laws on the subject of bankruptcies throughout the United States;

To coin money, regulate the value thereof, and of foreign coin, and fix the standard of weights and measures;

To provide for the punishment of counterfeiting the securities and current coin of the United States;

To establish post offices and post roads;

To promote the progress of science and useful arts, by securing for limited times to authors and inventors the exclusive right to their respective writings and discoveries;

To constitute tribunals inferior to the Supreme Court;

To define and punish piracies and felonies committed on the high seas, and offenses against the law of nations;

To declare war, grant letters of marque and reprisal, and make rules concerning captures on land and water;

To raise and support armies, **but no appropriation of money to that use shall be for a longer term than two years;**

To provide and maintain a navy;

To make rules for the government and regulation of the land and naval forces;

To provide for calling forth the militia to execute the laws of the union, suppress insurrections and repel invasions;

To provide for organizing, arming, and disciplining, the militia, and for governing such part of them as may be employed in the service of the United States, reserving to the states respectively, the appointment of the officers, and the authority of training the militia according to the discipline prescribed by Congress;

To exercise exclusive legislation in all cases whatsoever, over such District (not exceeding ten miles square) as may, by cession of particular states, and the acceptance of Congress, become the seat of the government of the United States, and to exercise like authority over all places purchased by the consent of the legislature of the state in which the same shall be, for the erection of forts, magazines, arsenals, dockyards, and other needful buildings;--And

To make all laws which shall be necessary and proper for carrying into execution the foregoing powers, and all other powers vested by this Constitution in the government of the United States, or in any department or officer thereof. (*Necessary and Proper Clause*)

Section 9. The migration or importation of such persons as any of the states now existing shall think proper to admit, shall not be prohibited by the Congress prior to the year one thousand eight hundred and eight, but a tax or duty may be imposed on such importation, not exceeding ten dollars for each person. (*Slave trade abolition*)

The privilege of **the writ of habeas corpus shall not be suspended,** unless when in cases of rebellion or invasion the public safety may require it.

No bill of attainder or ex post facto Law shall be passed. (*a law targeting a specific person for punishment without trial, or a law punishing an act already committed*)

No capitation, or other direct, tax shall be laid, unless in proportion to the census or enumeration herein before directed to be taken. (*Superceded by the 16th Amendment*)

No tax or duty shall be laid on articles exported from any state.

No preference shall be given by any regulation of commerce or revenue to the ports of one state over those of another: nor shall vessels bound to, or from, one state, be obliged to enter, clear or pay duties in another.

No money shall be drawn from the treasury, but in consequence of appropriations made by law; and a regular statement and account of receipts and expenditures of all public money shall be published from time to time.

No title of nobility shall be granted by the United States: and no person holding any office of profit or trust under them, shall, without the consent of the Congress, accept of any present, emolument, office, or title, of any kind whatever, from any king, prince, or foreign state.

Section 10. No state shall enter into any treaty, alliance, or confederation; grant letters of marque and reprisal; coin money; emit bills of credit; make anything but gold and silver coin a tender in payment of debts; pass any bill of attainder, ex post facto law, or law impairing the obligation of contracts, or grant any title of nobility.

No state shall, without the consent of the Congress, lay any imposts or duties on imports or exports, except what may be absolutely necessary for executing it's inspection laws: and the net produce of all duties and imposts, laid by any state on imports or exports, shall be for the use of the treasury of the United States; and all such laws shall be subject to the revision and control of the Congress.

No state shall, without the consent of Congress, lay any duty of tonnage, keep troops, or ships of war in time of peace, enter into any agreement or compact with another state, or with a foreign power, or engage in war, unless actually invaded, or in such imminent danger as will not admit of delay.

Article II (*Executive Branch*)

Section 1. The **executive power shall be vested in a President** of the United States of America. He shall hold his office during the term of four years, and, together with the Vice President, chosen for the same term, be elected, as follows:

Each state shall appoint, in such manner as the Legislature thereof may direct, a number of electors, equal to the whole number of Senators and Representatives to which the State may be entitled in the Congress: but no Senator or Representative, or person holding an office of trust or profit under the United States, shall be appointed an elector. (*Electoral College*)

The electors shall meet in their respective states, and vote by ballot for two persons, of whom one at least shall not be an inhabitant of the same state with themselves. And they shall make a list of all the persons voted for, and of the number of votes for each; which list they shall sign and certify, and transmit sealed to the seat of the government of the United States, directed to the President of the Senate. The President of the Senate shall, in the presence of the Senate and House of Representatives, open all the certificates, and the votes shall then be counted. **The person having the greatest number of votes shall be the President**, if such number be a majority of the whole number of electors appointed; and if there be more than one who have such majority, and have an equal number of votes, then the House of Representatives shall immediately choose by ballot one of them for President; and **if no person have a majority, then from the five highest on the list the said House shall in like manner choose the President**. But in choosing the President, the votes shall be taken by States, the representation from each state having one vote; A quorum for this purpose shall consist of a member or members from two thirds of the states, and a majority of all the states shall be necessary to a choice. In every case, after the choice of the President, the person having the greatest number of votes of the electors shall be the Vice President. But if there should remain two or more who have equal votes, the Senate shall choose from them by ballot the Vice President.

The Congress may determine the time of choosing the electors, and the day on which they shall give their votes; which day shall be the same throughout the United States.

No person except a natural born citizen, or a citizen of the United States, at the time of the adoption of this Constitution, shall be eligible to the office of President; neither shall any person be eligible to that office who shall not have attained to the age of **thirty five years**, and been fourteen Years a resident within the United States.

In case of the removal of the President from office, or of his death, resignation, or inability to discharge the powers and duties of the said office, the same shall devolve on the Vice President, and the Congress may by law provide for the case of removal, death, resignation or inability, both of the President and Vice President, declaring what officer shall then act as President, and such officer shall act accordingly, until the disability be removed, or a President shall be elected.

The President shall, at stated times, receive for his services, a compensation, which shall neither be increased nor diminished during the period for which he shall have been elected, and he shall not receive within that period any other emolument from the United States, or any of them.

Before he enter on the execution of his office, he shall take the following oath or affirmation:—"I do solemnly swear (or affirm) that I will faithfully execute the office of President of the United States, and will to the best of my ability, preserve, protect and defend the Constitution of the United States."

Section 2. The President shall be **commander in chief of the Army and Navy** of the United States, and of the militia of the several states, when called into the actual service of the United States; he may require the opinion, in writing, of the principal officer in each of the executive departments, upon any subject relating to the duties of their respective offices, and he shall have power to grant reprieves and pardons for offenses against the United States, except in cases of impeachment.

He shall have power, by and with the advice and consent of the Senate, to **make treaties, provided two thirds of the Senators present concur**; and he shall nominate, and by and with the advice and consent of the Senate, shall appoint **ambassadors**, other public ministers and consuls, **judges of the Supreme Court**, and all other officers of the United States, whose appointments are not herein otherwise provided for, and which shall be established by law: but the Congress may by law vest the appointment of such inferior officers, as they think proper, in the President alone, in the courts of law, or in the heads of departments.

The President shall have power to fill up all vacancies that may happen during the recess of the Senate, by granting commissions which shall expire at the end of their next session.

Section 3. He shall from time to time give to the Congress information of the **state of the union**, and recommend to their consideration such measures as he shall judge necessary and expedient; he may, on extraordinary occasions, convene both Houses, or either of them, and in case of disagreement between them, with respect to the time of adjournment, he may adjourn them to such time as he shall think proper; he shall receive ambassadors and other public ministers; he shall take care that the laws be faithfully executed, and shall commission all the officers of the United States.

Section 4. The President, Vice President and all civil officers of the United States, shall be removed from office on **impeachment** for, and conviction of, treason, bribery, or other high crimes and misdemeanors.

Article III (*Judicial Branch*)

Section 1. The **judicial power** of the United States, shall be vested in one Supreme Court, and in such inferior courts as the Congress may from time to time ordain and establish. The judges, both of the supreme and inferior courts, shall hold their offices during good behaviour, and shall, at stated times, receive for their services, a compensation, which shall not be diminished during their continuance in office.

Section 2. The judicial power shall extend to all cases, in law and equity, arising under this Constitution, the laws of the United States, and treaties made, or which shall be made, under their authority;—to all cases affecting ambassadors, other public ministers and consuls;— to all cases of admiralty and maritime jurisdiction;—to controversies to which the United States shall be a party;—to controversies between two or more states;—between a state and citizens of another state;—between citizens of different states;—between citizens of the same state claiming lands under grants of different states, and between a state, or the citizens thereof, and foreign states, citizens or subjects.

In all cases affecting ambassadors, other public ministers and consuls, and those in which a state shall be party, the Supreme Court shall have **original jurisdiction**. In all the other cases before mentioned, the Supreme Court shall have appellate jurisdiction, both as to law and fact, **with such exceptions, and under such regulations as the Congress shall make**.

The trial of all crimes, except in cases of impeachment, **shall be by jury**; and such trial shall be held in the state where the said crimes shall have been committed; but when not committed within any state, the trial shall be at such place or places as the Congress may by law have directed.

Section 3. Treason against the United States, shall consist only in levying war against them, or in adhering to their enemies, giving them aid and comfort. No person shall be convicted of treason unless on the testimony of **two witnesses to the same overt act**, or on confession in open court.

The Congress shall have power to declare the punishment of treason, but no attainder of treason shall work **corruption of blood**, or forfeiture except during the life of the person attainted. (corruption of blood is an old European concept that guilt could be passed on to the next generation; the American view is that individuals do not carry the sins of their parents)

Article IV (*Interstate Relations*)

Section 1. Full faith and credit shall be given in each state to the public acts, records, and judicial proceedings of every other state. And the Congress may by general laws prescribe the manner in which such acts, records, and proceedings shall be proved, and the effect thereof.

Section 2. The citizens of each state shall be entitled to all privileges and immunities of citizens in the several states.

A person charged in any state with treason, felony, or other crime, who shall flee from justice, and be found in another state, shall on demand of the executive authority of the state from which he fled, be delivered up, to be removed to the state having jurisdiction of the crime.

No person held to service or labor in one state, under the laws thereof, escaping into another, shall, in consequence of any law or regulation therein, be discharged from such service or labor, but shall be delivered up on claim of the party to whom such service or labor may be due. (*Fugitive Slave Clause superseded by 13th Amendment*)

Section 3. New states may be admitted by the Congress into this union; but no new states shall be formed or erected within the jurisdiction of any other state; nor any state be formed by the junction of two or more states, or parts of states, without the consent of the legislatures of the states concerned as well as of the Congress.

The Congress shall have power to dispose of and make all needful rules and regulations respecting the territory or other property belonging to the United States; and nothing in this Constitution shall be so construed as to prejudice any claims of the United States, or of any particular state.

Section 4. The United States shall guarantee to every state in this union **a republican form of government**, and shall protect each of them against invasion; and on application of the legislature, or of the executive (when the legislature cannot be convened) against domestic violence.

Article V (*Amendment*)

The Congress, whenever two thirds of both houses shall deem it necessary, shall propose **amendments to this Constitution**, or, on the application of the legislatures of two thirds of the several states, shall call a convention for proposing amendments, which, in either case, shall be valid to all intents and purposes, as part of this Constitution, **when ratified by the legislatures of three fourths of the several states**, or by conventions in three fourths thereof, as the one or the other mode of ratification may be proposed by the Congress; provided that no amendment which may be made prior to the year one thousand eight hundred and eight shall in any manner affect the first and fourth clauses in the ninth section of the first article; and that no state, without its consent, shall be deprived of its equal suffrage in the Senate.

Article VI (*Nation as a Whole*)

All debts contracted and engagements entered into, before the adoption of this Constitution, shall be as valid against the United States under this Constitution, as under the Confederation.

This Constitution, and the laws of the United States which shall be made in pursuance thereof; and all treaties made, or which shall be made, under the authority of the United States, **shall be the supreme law of the land**; and the judges in every state shall be bound thereby, anything in the Constitution or laws of any State to the contrary notwithstanding. (*Supremacy Clause*)

The Senators and Representatives before mentioned, and the members of the several state legislatures, and all executive and judicial officers, both of the United States and of the several states, shall be bound by oath or affirmation, to support this Constitution; but **no religious test shall ever be required** as a qualification to any office or public trust under the United States.

Article VII (*Ratification*)

The Ratification of the Conventions of nine States, shall be sufficient for the Establishment of this Constitution between the States so ratifying the Same.

THE BILL OF RIGHTS AND AMENDMENTS

(The Preamble to the Bill of Rights, or Amendments One through Ten, enacted in 1791, appears below, as written and passed by the 1st Congress; it is often not included as an explicit part of the Constitution, as it was not ratified by the states.)

Congress of the United States begun and held at the City of New-York, on Wednesday the fourth of March, one thousand seven hundred and eighty nine.

THE Conventions of a number of the States, having at the time of their adopting the Constitution, expressed a desire, **in order to prevent misconstruction or abuse of its powers, that further declaratory and restrictive clauses should be added**: And as extending the ground of public confidence in the Government, will best ensure the beneficent ends of its institution.

RESOLVED by the Senate and House of Representatives of the United States of America, in Congress assembled, two thirds of both Houses concurring, that the following Articles be proposed to the Legislatures of the several States, as amendments to the Constitution of the United States, all, or any of which Articles, when ratified by three fourths of the said Legislatures, to be valid to all intents and purposes, as part of the said Constitution; viz.

ARTICLES in addition to, and Amendment of the Constitution of the United States of America, proposed by Congress, and ratified by the Legislatures of the several States, pursuant to the fifth Article of the original Constitution.

Amendment I

Congress shall make no law respecting an **establishment of religion**, or **prohibiting the free exercise thereof**; or abridging the freedom of **speech**, or of the **press**; or the right of the people peaceably to **assemble**, and to **petition** the government for a redress of grievances.

Amendment II

A well regulated militia, being necessary to the security of a free state, the right of the people to **keep and bear arms**, shall not be infringed.

Amendment III

No soldier shall, in time of peace be quartered in any house, without the consent of the owner, nor in time of war, but in a manner to be prescribed by law.

Amendment IV

The right of the people to be secure in their persons, houses, papers, and effects, against **unreasonable searches and seizures**, shall not be violated, and no warrants shall issue, but upon probable cause, supported by oath or affirmation, and particularly describing the place to be searched, and the persons or things to be seized.

Amendment V

No person shall be held to answer for a capital, or otherwise infamous crime, unless on a presentment or indictment of a **grand jury**, except in cases arising in the land or naval forces, or in the militia, when in actual service in time of war or public danger; nor shall any person be subject for the same offense to be **twice put in jeopardy** of life or limb; nor shall be compelled in any criminal case to be a **witness against himself**, nor be **deprived of life, liberty, or property, without due process of law**; nor shall **private property be taken for public use**, without just compensation.

Amendment VI

In all criminal prosecutions, the accused shall enjoy the right to a **speedy and public trial**, by an impartial **jury** of the state and district wherein the crime shall have been committed, which district shall have been previously ascertained by law, and to be informed of the nature and cause of the accusation; to be confronted with the witnesses against him; to have compulsory process for obtaining witnesses in his favor, and to have the assistance of **counsel for his defense**.

Amendment VII

In suits at common law, where the value in controversy shall exceed twenty dollars, the right of **trial by jury** shall be preserved, and no fact tried by a jury, shall be otherwise reexamined in any court of the United States, than according to the rules of the common law.

Amendment VIII

Excessive bail shall not be required, nor excessive fines imposed, nor **cruel and unusual punishments** inflicted.

Amendment IX

The enumeration in the Constitution, of certain **rights**, shall not be construed to deny or disparage **others retained by the people**.

Amendment X

The powers not delegated to the United States by the Constitution, nor prohibited by it to the states, are **reserved to the states respectively, or to the people**.

Amendment XIII (*1865*)

Section 1. Neither slavery nor involuntary servitude, except as a punishment for crime whereof the party shall have been duly convicted, shall exist within the United States, or any place subject to their jurisdiction.

Section 2. Congress shall have power to enforce this article by appropriate legislation.

Amendment XIV (*1868*)

Section 1. All persons born or naturalized in the United States, and subject to the jurisdiction thereof, are citizens of the United States and of the state wherein they reside. No state shall make or enforce any law which shall abridge the **privileges or immunities** of citizens of the United States; nor shall any state deprive any person of life, liberty, or property, without **due process** of law; nor deny to any person within its jurisdiction the **equal protection** of the laws.

Section 2. Representatives shall be apportioned among the several states according to their respective numbers, counting the whole number of persons in each state, excluding Indians not taxed. But when the right to vote at any election for the choice of electors for President and Vice President of the United States, Representatives in Congress, the executive and judicial officers of a state, or the members of the legislature thereof, is denied to any of the male inhabitants of such state, being twenty-one years of age, and citizens of the United States, or in any way abridged, except for participation in rebellion, or other crime, the basis of representation therein shall be reduced in the proportion which the number of such male citizens shall bear to the whole number of male citizens twenty-one years of age in such state.

Section 3. No person shall be a Senator or Representative in Congress, or elector of President and Vice President, or hold any office, civil or military, under the United States, or under any state, who, having previously taken an oath, as a member of Congress, or as an officer of the United States, or as a member of any state legislature, or as an executive or judicial officer of any state, to support the Constitution of the United States, shall have engaged in insurrection or rebellion against the same, or given aid or comfort to the enemies thereof. But Congress may by a vote of two-thirds of each House, remove such disability.

Section 4. The validity of the public debt of the United States, authorized by law, including debts incurred for payment of pensions and bounties for services in suppressing insurrection or rebellion, shall not be questioned. But neither the United States nor any state shall assume or pay any debt or obligation incurred in aid of insurrection or rebellion against the United States, or any claim for the loss or emancipation of any slave; but all such debts, obligations and claims shall be held illegal and void.

Section 5. The Congress shall have power to enforce, by appropriate legislation, the provisions of this article.

Amendment XV (*1870*)

Section 1. The right of citizens of the United States to vote shall not be denied or abridged by the United States or by any state on account of race, color, or previous condition of servitude.

Section 2. The Congress shall have power to enforce this article by appropriate legislation.

Amendment XVI (*1913*)

The Congress shall have power to lay and collect **taxes on incomes**, from whatever source derived, without apportionment among the several States, and without regard to any census or enumeration.

Amendment XVII (*1913*)

The Senate of the United States shall be composed of two **Senators** from each State, **elected by the people thereof**, for six years; and each Senator shall have one vote. The electors in each State shall have the qualifications requisite for electors of the most numerous branch of the State legislatures.

When vacancies happen in the representation of any State in the Senate, the executive authority of such State shall issue writs of election to fill such vacancies: Provided, That the legislature of any State may empower the executive thereof to make temporary appointments until the people fill the vacancies by election as the legislature may direct.

This amendment shall not be so construed as to affect the election or term of any Senator chosen before it becomes valid as part of the Constitution.

Amendment XIX (*1920*)

The right of citizens of the United States to **vote** shall not be denied or abridged by the United States or by any State **on account of sex**.

Congress shall have power to enforce this article by appropriate legislation.

Amendment XXVI (*1971*)

The right of citizens of the United States, who are **eighteen years of age or older, to vote** shall not be denied or abridged by the United States or by any State on account of age. Congress shall have the power to enforce this law through appropriate legislation.

NOTES

1. When considering a case before the Supreme Court, you can tell who won the case in the lower court by the order of the names. The person bringing the appeal goes first in the order, so the *first* name is the previous loser, while the *second* name is the previous winner.
2. In the 2010–2011 term, the Court expanded the protections afforded to minors, ruling that age must now be taken into consideration to determine if detention by authorities or a criminal confession is perceived to be voluntary, because "children characteristically lack the capacity to exercise mature judgment and possess only an incomplete ability to understand the world around them" (*JDB v. North Carolina*, 2010).
3. A student of mine once got into a public argument with a professor of American History about whether the phrase "all men are created equal" was in the Constitution. Having just discussed this in my course, the student corrected the professor about the origin of the phrase. The professor insisted that obviously the student was wrong and everyone knows that this phrase can be found in the Constitution.
4. The book's original title is actually *The Life and Strange Surprizing Adventures of Robinson Crusoe, of York, Mariner: Who lived Eight and Twenty Years, all alone in an un-inhabited Island on the Coast of America, near the Mouth of the Great River of Oroonoque; Having been cast on Shore by Shipwreck, wherein all the Men perished but himself. With An Account how he was at last as strangely deliver'd by Pyrates.*
5. Akhil Amar, *The Bill of Rights* (New Haven: Yale University Press, 1998), xi, 125.
6. Alexander Bickel, *The Least Dangerous Branch* (New York: Bobbs-Merrill, 1962), 12.
7. Each of these ways of reading has many living backers and published books in its corner. The first is traditional or pre-modern criticism, which was more popular before the rise of post-modern disbelief in verifiable knowledge. The second approach is associated with what is called formalism, while the third is often termed reception theory. The final approach is sometimes called poststructuralist or sometimes deconstructionist, but whatever the term, it emphasizes the fundamental ambiguity of a text. In this view, a text can have different

meanings to different readers, which means that the project of nailing down a specific meaning, whether inherent in the author's intent, or in the text, or in previous authoritative readings, is impossible. Deconstructionists believe that this project is at best wrong-headed and at worst fascist; more traditional scholars see the post-modern or deconstructionist movement as gutting the important content of books, or turning meaning into mush.

8. All of our states have a highest court, usually called the X Supreme Court or Supreme Court of X, though some employ other names such as the Supreme Judicial Court (in Maine and Massachusetts), or the Supreme Court of Appeals (in West Virginia). In Maryland and New York the highest court is called the Court of Appeals. In New York, the Supreme Court is the name for the actual trial court in which criminal defendants face a jury. This creates a problem for many American citizens who gain most of their legal knowledge from watching *Law & Order*, which always prefaces its trials by announcing that they are in the Supreme Court. I am still surprised every time I see this, even after countless episodes.

9. In *Cooper v. Telfair* (1800) Justice Chase ruled that "It is indeed a general opinion, it is expressly admitted by all this bar, and some of the Judges have, individually, in the Circuits, decided that the Supreme Court can declare an act of Congress to be unconstitutional, and therefore, invalid; but there is no adjudication of the Supreme Court itself upon the point."

Two years later in *Calder v. Bull* the Court continued that "If any act of Congress, or of the Legislature of a State violates those constitutional provisions, it is unquestionably void; though I admit, as the authority to declare it void is of a delicate and awful nature, the Court will never resort to that authority, but in a clear and urgent case."

10. *Federalist Papers*, 1998. Penguin Classics Edition edited by Clinton Rossiter, 466.

11. "Whoever attentively considers the different departments of power must perceive, that, in a government in which they are separated from each other, the judiciary, from the nature of its functions, will always be the least dangerous to the political rights of the Constitution; because it will be least in a capacity to annoy or injure them. The Executive not only dispenses the honors, but holds the sword of the community. The legislature not only commands the purse, but prescribes the rules by which the duties and rights of every citizen are to be regulated. The judiciary, on the contrary, has no influence over either the sword or the purse; no direction either of the strength or of the wealth of the society; and can take no active resolution whatever. It may truly be said to have neither FORCE nor WILL, but merely judgment; and must ultimately depend upon the aid of the executive arm even for the efficacy of its judgments."

12. Bickel, *Least Dangerous Branch*, 58, 24.

13. This position is sometimes called the *Doctrine of the Clear Mistake*, traced to an influential 1893 essay by the legal scholar James Bradley Thayer ("The Origin and Scope of the American Doctrine of Constitutional Law" 7 *Harvard Law Review* 129: the Court should declare a law unconstitutional only "when those who have the right to make laws have not merely made a mistake, but have made a very clear one" [p. 144]).

14. See the Fourteenth Amendment: "No State shall make or enforce any law which shall abridge the privileges or immunities of citizens of the United States," and *Black's Law Dictionary*, 6th edition: "A power, privilege, or immunity guaranteed under a constitution, statutes or decisional laws, or claimed as a result of long usage."

15. It may strike some readers as ironic to cite Lincoln as an authority for federalism. It isn't. Federalism is not about secession, or the idea that states are sovereign entities that entered the union at will and can leave at will. It is about limited national power within a permanent union of the people and the states, maintaining a delicate balance. Lincoln argued clearly that the federal government had little power over the workings within individual states, but only the *national* power to maintain the union.

16. Edmund Burke, *Letter to Sheriffs*, Part II, page 274; *Reflections*, Part IV, page 272, in *The Works of the Right Honourable Edmund Burke*. London: Henry G. Bohn, 1856

17. Ibid., *Reflections*, Part IV, 7.

18. In some senses we still see rights as dependent on fulfilling responsibilities, at least the responsibility to not commit serious crimes, which is why convicted felons cannot vote. They have broken the social contract and proven that they are not public-spirited, and so have permanently lost certain political rights. This is not a *positive responsibility* to do anything in order to have the right to vote, but is at least a *negative responsibility* to not commit a major crime (misdemeanors do not count, or the voting population would be severely limited).

19. See http://www.youtube.com/watch?v=SQdDjBAJt7c

20. *Jacobson v. Massachusetts* (1905) 197 U.S. 14

21. Ibid., 22

22. Ibid.

23. Bickel, *Least Dangerous Branch*, 36.

24. *Fay v. New York* (1947) 332 U.S. 282

25. *Poe v. Ullman* (1961) 367 U.S. 540, 543

26. Letter to John B. Colvin, 29 September 1810, *Works of Thomas Jefferson*, Volume 11, 146. See http://press-pubs.uchicago.edu/founders/documents/a2_3s8.html.

27. *Kennedy v. Mendoza-Martinez* (1963) 372 U.S. 160

28. *Dennis v. U.S.* (1951) 341 U.S. 509

29. *Olmstead v. New York* (1928) 277 U.S. 478

30. *Griswold v. Connecticut* (1965) 381 U.S. 483, 484

31. *Lawrence v. Texas* (2003) 539 U.S. 562, 578-79

32. The speaker was Manfred Ewald, head of East German sports during the era of forced doping and sex reassignment (men competing as women in order to win medals). He was put on trial in 2000, convicted, given a 22 month suspended sentence, and died in 2002.

33. See *Black's Law Dictionary*, 7th edition: "So far as legal theory is concerned, a person is any being whom the law regards as capable of rights and duties. Any being that is so capable is a person, whether a human being or not, and no being that is not so capable is a person, even though he be a man. Persons are

the substances of which rights and duties are the attributes" (quoting Salmond *Jurisprudence* 1947).

34. See Title 1 of the U.S Code: "In determining the meaning of any Act of Congress ... the words "person" and "whoever" include corporations, companies, associations, firms, partnerships, societies, and joint stock companies, as well as individuals" (1 USC §1). See also the 2010 ruling in *Citizens United v. FEC*, which expands the free speech rights of corporations. The majority "rejected the argument that political speech of corporations or other associations should be treated differently under the First Amendment simply because such associations are not 'natural persons.'" The dissenters believed "the conceit that corporations must be treated identically to natural persons in the political sphere is not only inaccurate but also inadequate," because "the distinctions between corporate and human speakers is significant" (Justice Kennedy for the majority, p. 26; Justice Stevens for the dissent, p. 2).

35. *Bradwell v. Illinois* (1873), concurrence of Bradley, Swayne, and Field, upholding the Illinois ban on admission of women to practice law (83 U.S. 130).

36. *Muller v. Oregon* (1908) 208 U.S. 420

37. *Craig v. Boren* (1976) 429 U.S. 198

38. *U.S. v. Virginia* (1996) 518 U.S. 516

39. *Dred Scott v. Sandford* (1857) 60 U.S. 407

40. *Brown v. Board of Education of Topeka* (1954) 347 U.S. 490

41. *Muller v. Oregon*, 421–22

42. *Planned Parenthood v. Casey* (1992) 505 U.S. 866

43. *Brown v. Plata* (2011) 131 S.Ct. 1954

44. *Planned Parenthood v. Casey*, 835, 855, 836

45. *Dickerson v. United States* (2000) 530 U.S. 443

46. *Collected Works of Abraham Lincoln*, Volume 4 (New Brunswick: Rutgers University Press, 1953) 168–9.

47. On the shifting significance of the Declaration, see Gary Wills' influential book *Lincoln at Gettysburg*.

48. *Lawrence v. Texas*, 560

49. Antonin Scalia, *A Matter of Interpretation* (Princeton University Press, 1997), 32.

50. *Lochner v. New York* (1905) 198 U.S. 45

51. Scalia, *Matter of Interpretation*, 20

52. Learned Hand, quoted in Bickel, *Least Dangerous Branch*, 23.

53. *Planned Parenthood v. Casey*, 844

54. Ibid., 993

55. Woodrow Wilson, *Constitutional Government in the United States* (Columbia University Press, 1908), 56.

56. Oliver Wendell Holmes, Jr., *The Common Law* (Boston: Little, Brown and Company, 1881), 1.

57. *Planned Parenthood v. Casey*, 877

58. Ibid., 987

59. See Jack Rakove, *Original Meanings* (New York: Vintage, 1996), 353.

60, *McCulloch v. Maryland* (1819) 17 U.S. 407, 415

61. *Gibbons v. Ogden* (1824) 22 U.S. 188

62. *South Carolina v. U.S.* (1905) 199 U.S. 448
63. Henry Hazlitt, "Our Obsolete Constitution" *Reader's Digest* April 1931: 1099.
64. Thurgood Marshall (1987) "The Constitution: A Living Document" 30 *Howard Law Journal* 915.
65. *Trop v. Dulles* (1958) 356 U.S. 101
66. *Furman v. Georgia* (1972) 408 U.S. 360
67. Ibid., 362
68. Ibid., 363
69. *Gregg v. Georgia* (1976) 428 U.S. 232
70. *Trop v. Dulles,* 102
71. *Lawrence v. Texas* (2003) 539 U.S. 560
72. Ibid., 539 U.S. 562
73. For the purposes of the legal proceeding, McCorvey claimed the pregnancy was the product of a rape, but later admitted that this was not the case. In a strange twist that reflects the divisive politics of abortion in America, McCorvey later became a pro-life activist.
74. *Roe v. Wade* (1973) 410 U.S. 155
75. *Griswold v. Connecticut* (1965) recognizes a right to privacy in regard to intimate marital relations, especially contraception; *Pierce v. Society of Sisters* (1925) protects the right to educate children as parents see fit; and *Mapp v. Ohio* (1961) upholds Fourth Amendment protections against unreasonable searches of the home.
76. *Roe v. Wade,* 156-57
77. Ibid., 133
78. Ibid., 158, 159
79. "With respect to the State's important and legitimate interest in potential life, the 'compelling' point is at viability. This is so because the fetus then presumably has the capability of meaningful life outside the mother's womb" (410 U.S. 163). Justice Blackmun clarified his position sixteen years later in his dissent in *Webster*: "The viability line reflects the biological facts and truths of fetal development; it marks that threshold moment prior to which a fetus cannot survive separate from the woman and cannot reasonably and objectively be regarded as a subject of rights or interests distinct from, or paramount to, those of the pregnant woman. At the same time, the viability standard takes account of the undeniable fact that as the fetus evolves into its postnatal form, and as it loses its dependence on the uterine environment, the State's interest in the fetus' potential human life, and in fostering a regard for human life in general, becomes compelling" (492 U.S. 553).
80. *Roe v. Wade,* 116
81. *Planned Parenthood v. Casey,* 979
82. *Brown v. Plata* (2011) 131 S.Ct. 1958-9
83. Ibid., 131 S.Ct. 1928
84. Ibid., 131 S.Ct. 1965, 1966, 1968
85. *Wal-Mart v. Dukes* (2011) 131 S.Ct. 2552
86. Ibid., 131 S.Ct. 2555
87. Ibid., 131 S.Ct. 2563-4

87. *NFIB v. Sebelius* (2012) 567 U.S. 6, 2, 3
89. Ibid., 18, 18, 20
90. Ibid., 23
91. Ibid., 51, 52, 57
92. Scalia dissent, 2
93. Ginsburg dissent, 2, 15, 36–37
94. Ibid., 9. Scalia's conclusion puts the dispute in even more clear focus: "The constitutional protections that this case involves are protections of structure. Structural protections—notably, the restraints imposed by federalism and separation of powers—are less romantic and have less obvious connection to personal freedoms than the provisions of the Bill of Rights or the Civil War Amendments. Hence they tend to be undervalued or even forgotten by our citizens. It should be the responsibility of the Court to teach otherwise, to remind our people that the Framers considered structural protections of freedom the most important ones, for which reason they alone were embodied in the original Constitution and not left to later amendment. The fragmentation of power produced by the structure of our Government is central to liberty, and when we destroy it, we place liberty at peril."
95. *NFIB v. Sebelius*, 31, 31
96. Ibid., 31, 32, 32, 45
97. Ibid., 33
98. Scalia dissent 17, 18, 27–28
99. "The unique attributes of the health-care market render everyone active in that market." Ginsburg dissent, 28
100. Ibid., 5
101. Ibid., 6, 7
102. Ibid., 22
103. Scalia dissent, 12
104. *NFIB v. Sebelius*, 58

INDEX